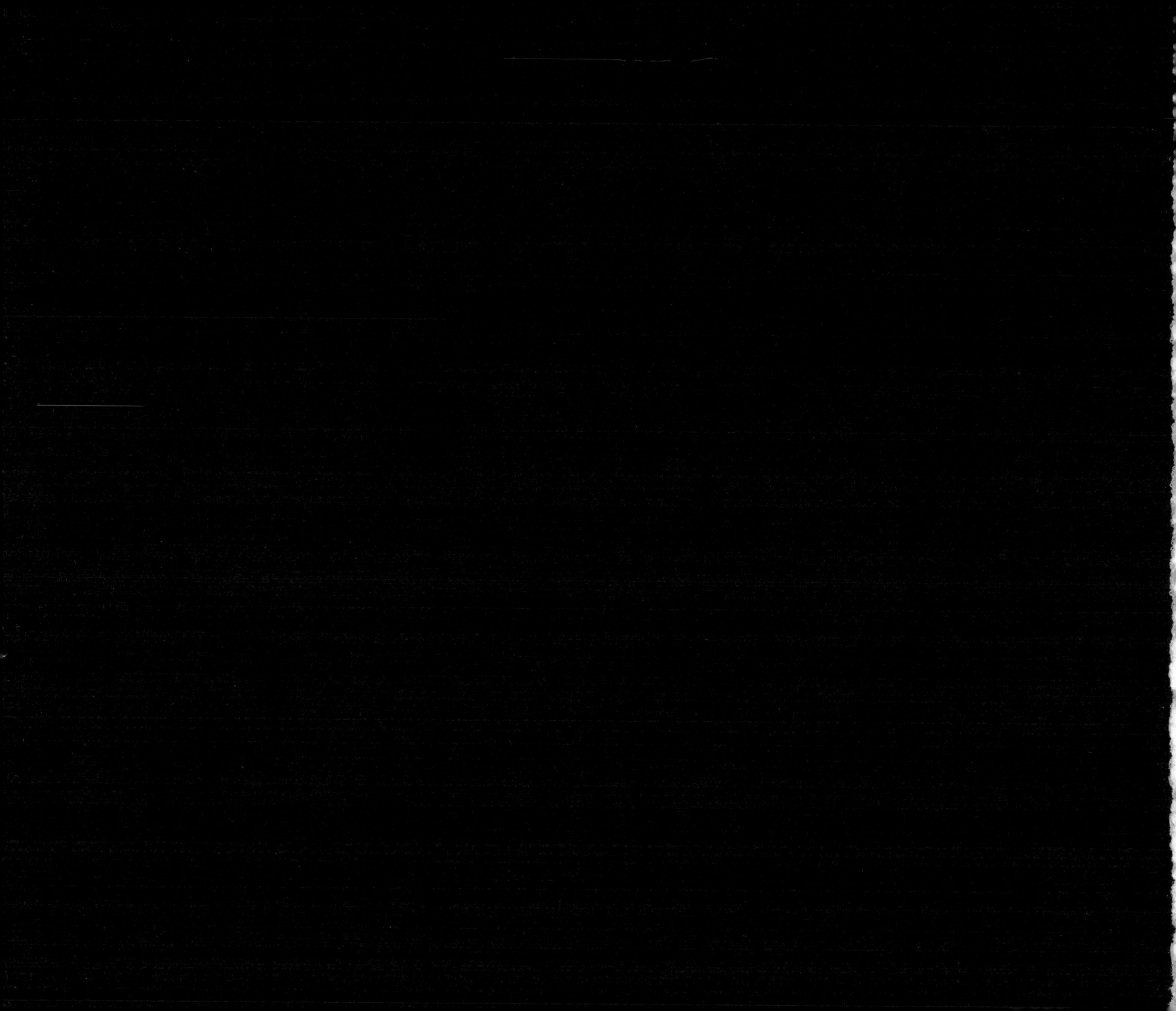

All We Like Sheep

A Family Tabletop Devotional

To Tony & Tracy!
May the Good
Shepherd Lead you
Beside Still Waters

Tommy Walker
Cor 3:17

All we like sheep have gone astray; we have turned to our own way;
and the Lord hath laid on Him the iniquities of us all.

ISAIAH 53:6

All We Like Sheep

A Family Tabletop Devotional

SECOND PRINTING

Dr. Larry F. Guthrie

Robert C. Newhouse

All We Like Sheep

A Family Tabletop Devotional Series

Managing Editors: Larry Guthrie, Robert Newhouse
Art Director/Graphic Design: Zyrek Castelino
Design Consultants: Paul Gilmer, Scott Linke, Laura DeMasie
Copy Editors: Paul Molitor, Lois Guthrie, Donna Rees
Publishing Director: Paul Molitor
Image Editor: Eric Vest

All Scripture quotations are taken from the Holy Bible, King James version.
All Scripture definitions are taken from Online Bible Software,
www.online-bible.com/maconlinebible.html.

Printed in the United States of America
ISBN 978-1-4507-6548-0

Photo Credits

EVP = © Copyright, Eric Vest Photography, LLC, 2011
www.ericvestphotography.com
IND = Independent Photographer
SS = Used under license from Shutterstock.com

TABLE OF CONTENTS

AUTHORS' PREFACE

I'm Larry. I teach by telling stories and painting pictures. It's the same way that ancient Hebrews passed down important lessons from generation to generation. It's the way Jesus taught. He told stories and painted pictures.

For example, instead of saying that it is important for a man to build a firm foundation that will resist the pressures of this world, He said, *"I will liken him to a wise man, which built his house upon a rock. And the rain descended, and the floods came, and the winds blew and beat upon that house; and it fell not"* (Matthew 7:24–27).

As you look at each chapter, study the picture. Look for details. Ask questions. Attempt to understand the messages hidden in these carefully chosen photos. Read the text and dig for the underlying personal applications. Consider the many words that have double meanings. Above all, share what you see and hear with the rest of your family.

May the Lord bless the time you spend together as a family as you read this book, and may He give you insights beyond those that we have shared here.

—Larry

I'm Bob. I teach by linking concepts and ideas together. That's what Paul did in his epistles.

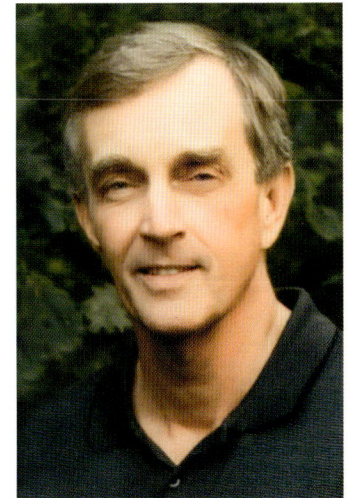

I see God's Word as a treasure map directing us to hidden jewels found buried beneath the surface. I begin digging for treasure in Scripture by assuming that the words translated into English mean something more in their original language than what they seem to mean in English. The Hebrew language is full of imagery, and Greek is so precise that if we don't dig into these original languages for meaning, we'll miss the full depth and richness of insight they offer. As we search for these treasures, God will show us how all Scripture is linked together and points us to Jesus Christ.

Whether you study God's Creation or His Word, they both reveal the glory of Jesus Christ. He is the real Treasure that we seek.

As you read these chapters together as a family, I pray that your hearts will be transformed as God reveals Himself to you. God has personally taught me so much while working on this book, and I have been wonderfully blessed by working with Larry and sharing what I've learned with you!

—Bob

HOW TO USE THIS BOOK

All We Like Sheep is intended to serve families as they meet around a table, a fireplace, or in their family room. It is a tabletop book with lots of photographs and plenty to look at and think about.

All We Like Sheep is meant to be read together as a family. It is to be read slowly. It's intended to elicit discussion, raise questions, and stimulate interaction among family members. The photographs are carefully selected to amplify the text. "A picture is worth a thousand words," so make sure you talk about the photographs and discover how each one reinforces the message in the devotional. The authors anticipate that it may take a month to read and discuss the book's twenty chapters.

Parents are encouraged to read several pages ahead of their family and to prayerfully consider how the Lord might tailor the family's review of each chapter to meet the particular needs of their family. Don't just read the pages. It is important to dig deeper than what is written on the page. Look for personal applications, and prayerfully ponder one another's thoughts and ideas. Let one comment lead to another and another and another.

All We Like Sheep builds on the words of Paul, who wrote, *"For the invisible things of him from the creation of the world are clearly seen, being understood by the things that are made, even his eternal power and Godhead; so that they are without excuse" (Romans 1:20).* By looking at God's creation we catch a glimpse of His attributes. The purpose of this book is to unveil the wonderful lessons hidden in God's creation. However, the authors' words and pictures only highlight the Word of God. They should not replace God's Word. Please take the time to slowly read the Bible verses in the chapters. Let God's Word sink deep into your soul, and listen to what He is saying to you. Let the chapters of this book clarify and deepen your understanding of the Word.

Each chapter also includes opposing character qualities and their definitions. One represents the positive aspect of the lesson and the other represents the negative. We've given these character qualities names and definitions in order to help you communicate with one another. Use them as "handles" to apply the concepts in your everyday life.

Finally, when you close the pages of this book, it is our prayer that you will take the stories, pictures, and concepts with you as you walk through your day together as a family. Please take seriously the words of Moses as he commanded the Israelites, saying: *"And ye shall teach them your children, speaking of them when thou sittest in thine house, and when thou walkest by the way, when thou liest down, and when thou risest up. . . . that your days may be multiplied . . . as the days of heaven upon the earth" (Deuteronomy 11:19–21).*

ACKNOWLEDGEMENTS

This Tabletop Family Devotional is a dream come true for me. For years I have wanted to share the stories and lessons the Lord has written on my heart. The fulfillment of this dream is the result of the Lord's persistent encouragement and prodding. It is also the result of the contributions of countless individuals who have influenced the compilation of this message in many ways.

First of all I want to thank my dear wife, Lois. She has patiently and courageously shared her heart with me through the whole journey. Special thanks go to my daughter and son-in-law, Mike and Becky Poulos, who founded Harvest Home Farm ministries, where many of the photos and experiences for this book originated. Special recognition goes to Zyrek Castelino, Laura DeMasie, and Donna Rees for their expertise with design and editing.

I also appreciate the mentoring and training of Dr. Bill Gothard, who has shepherded me for many years. Finally, my greatest praise is to the Lord Jesus Christ, who gave me the grace to share these lessons with you. I'm reminded daily that Jesus said, "*For without me you can do nothing*" (*John 15:5b*).

—Larry

First I'd like to thank Larry Guthrie for sharing with me his audio devotions titled "Food for Thought." I would daily forward these delightful devotionals to the TEACH families with a brief commentary. Soon the comments became more detailed as God opened up His Word. When Larry asked if I'd like to collaborate with him to write a book, using those commentaries, I was surprised, honored, and humbled.

I'd like to thank my children (Jonathon, Jeremy, Sarah, Marija, and Joseph) for the more than twenty years we had daily family devotions together in which we studied God's Word, asked thousands of questions, and had delightful discussions as we searched together for answers. Many of the insights in this book were discovered during these *"days of heaven upon the earth" (Deuteronomy 11:21)*. I'm also indebted to Dr. Bill Gothard and his ATI program for teaching us all how to dig into God's Word and find Treasure. I'm grateful to the TEACH Board of Directors, John and Bonnie Anderson, Kathy Pinson, and Jeff Belden, who encouraged me to take the time to record these thoughts.

Above all, I'd like to thank my lovely wife, Bethany, for showing me God's unconditional love through the faithful, undying support she has given me for thirty-five years. Bethany, I love you more every day, and I thank God for you.

—Bob

I Shall Not Want

The other day I moved our flock of sheep to a new pasture, but I forgot to turn on the electric fence. Without exception the sheep headed for the edge of the pasture, preferring the grass outside the fence to the lush grass inside.

It was only after I turned the electricity on that the grass outside the fence lost its attractiveness.

When the Psalmist wrote, *"The Lord is my shepherd, I shall not want,"* I'm convinced that he was talking about the fact that sheep always want what they don't have. To them the grass is always greener on the other side of the fence. Isn't that so true of us as well? We want whatever it is that we don't have. We want what our neighbors have. But when the Lord is our Shepherd, we can be content. We can say, "I shall not want more than what He provides."

—Larry

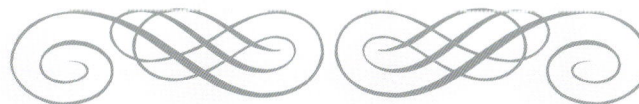

Contentment is choosing to be satisfied with the grass on your side of the fence.

Greed is wanting more than your Shepherd provides.

Do you ever think that the grass is greener on the other side of the fence? Larry says that's a common trait with sheep. When they look at the grass right below their noses, they can see how sparse it is; they notice the dirt and rocks between the blades. Because sheep are built low to the ground, when they view grass at a distance the blades blend together to appear thick, lush, and green. It's an optical illusion that the grass is greener over there. So, because it appears greener farther away, they are always trying to find a way to get to the grass on the other side of the fence.

Psalm 23 says that if the Lord is your Shepherd then *"[you] shall not want"* more than what you already have. You trust that your Good Shepherd knows what you need and you are content with what He has already provided for you.

WHY WASN'T EVE CONTENT IN THE GARDEN OF EDEN?

Who is it that makes you think that God is withholding something good from you? Didn't Satan sow those seeds of discontent in Eve's heart? God had placed a boundary around the tree of the knowledge of good and evil to protect Adam and Eve. Then He said that they could eat of every tree of

> *Satan is still trying to make us discontent with what God has already provided.*

the Garden except that one: *"Of every tree of the garden thou mayest freely eat: But of the tree of the knowledge of good and evil, thou shalt not eat of it: for in the day that thou eatest thereof thou shalt surely die"* (Genesis 2:16–17).

Satan was able to persuade Eve that God must be withholding something from her that would make her life better: *"For God doth know that in the day ye eat thereof, then your eyes shall be opened, and ye shall be as gods, knowing good and evil"* (Genesis 3:5).

Think about it. Eve was in the Garden of Eden—paradise on earth in the presence of God. And even there, Satan convinced her that she lacked something. Just like Larry's sheep, she was soon convinced that the fruit was better on the other side of the fence.

Satan told Eve that she could become like God by eating the fruit that was forbidden to her. Why was that tempting to Eve? Wasn't she already like God? Hadn't God already made her in His image? The Garden of Eden was heaven on earth, but still she listened to Satan's lies, and soon the forbidden fruit became more attractive than the fruit that God had already provided.

WHY WASN'T LUCIFER CONTENT IN HEAVEN?

How did the serpent so easily persuade Eve to be discontent with what she had? Perhaps because he had previously convinced himself to be discontent with what he had in heaven. In heaven, the serpent's name was Lucifer, which means "the light bearer." All the angels in heaven looked at him as he held the Light of God. But he was not content with that. He wanted to be like God. He wanted to be the light, not just the light-bearer. Since God is a jealous God and will not share His glory with another, He cast Lucifer out of heaven.

"How art thou fallen from heaven, O Lucifer, son of the morning! . . . For thou hast said in thine heart, I will ascend into heaven, I will exalt my throne above the stars of God: I will sit also upon the mount of the congregation, in the sides of the north: I will ascend above the heights of the clouds; I will be like the most High" (Isaiah 14:12–14).

WHO FOLLOWED LUCIFER OUT OF HEAVEN?

God didn't cast only Lucifer out of heaven that day. Somehow, Lucifer persuaded other angels to follow him, and they, too, were cast out. Think of how persuasive Satan must have been, to be able to deceive angels that were actually living in heaven. *"And the great dragon was cast out, that old serpent, called the Devil, and Satan, which deceiveth the whole world: he was cast out into the earth, and his angels were cast out with him" (Revelation 12:9).*

After Lucifer came to earth, he used the first chance he had to tempt Eve to be like God. The very thing that got Lucifer expelled from heaven also caused Adam and Eve to be driven from the Garden of Eden. When we read this, we're stunned that Eve could have been so foolish. How could she risk losing everything by stealing something she didn't even need? Perhaps you can identify with her struggle.

ARE YOU CONTENT WITH WHAT YOU HAVE?

God has already provided everything for us to be content in this life, and yet we are so easily persuaded to want something more. We believe that "more" will make our lives more fulfilled. But we don't need anything more. Jesus has already given us the abundant life: Himself! *"In Thy presence is fullness of joy; at Thy right hand there are pleasures for evermore" (Psalm 16:11).* In God's presence we can have peace and joy and love exactly where we are right now. Jesus is the abundant life, and when we are in His presence; we don't need anything more.

Satan is still trying to make us discontent with what God has already provided for us. Do you think that your life would be better if you were more popular? more wealthy? more powerful? having more fun? The abundant life doesn't require any of those things. God says: *"But godliness with contentment is great gain. . . . And having food and raiment let us be therewith content" (I Timothy 6:6–8).* *"Let your conversation be without covetousness; and be content with such things as ye have: for he hath said, I will never leave thee, nor forsake thee" (Hebrews 13:5).* *"O fear the LORD, ye his saints: for there is no want to them that fear him" (Psalm 34:9).*

As you read the following verses, ponder the thought that God has already provided everything needed for you to live the abundant life. The grass is not greener on the other side of the fence. May you have a day filled with contentment as you bask in the presence of God.

—Bob

"O fear the LORD, ye his saints: for there is no want to them that fear him. The young lions do lack, and suffer hunger: but they that seek the LORD shall not want any good thing. . . . A little that a righteous man hath is better than the riches of many wicked. . . . Better is little with the fear of the LORD than great treasure and trouble therewith. . . . Better is a little with righteousness than great revenues without right. . . . No good thing will he withhold from them that walk uprightly. . . . But rather seek ye the kingdom of God; and all these things shall be added unto you. Fear not, little flock; for it is your Father's good pleasure to give you the kingdom. . . . He that spared not his own Son, but delivered him up for us all, how shall he not with him also freely give us all things? . . . My God shall supply all your need according to his riches in glory by Christ Jesus."

Psalm 34:9–10, Psalm 37:16, Proverbs 15:16, Proverbs 16:8, Psalm 84:11, Luke 12:31–32, Romans 8:32, Philippians 4:19

CHAPTER TWO

Lying Down in
Green Pastures

Seeing a flock of sheep lying in a green pasture is perhaps one of the most peaceful sights I have ever witnessed.

For sheep, peace doesn't come easily. For sheep to lie down they must be completely free of worry. They simply will not lie down if they're troubled.

Peace doesn't come easily for us either. We worry about money. We're anxious about our health. We even fret about worrying so much. Paul writes in Philippians 4: "Don't be anxious about anything. Pray, pray with thanksgiving. Let God know your troubles. And His peace, the peace that transcends all understanding, will calm your mind."

This is the only peace that can conquer our fears. It's the peace that comes when we lay our burdens at the foot of the cross. It's then and only then that we, too, can lie down in green pastures.

—Larry

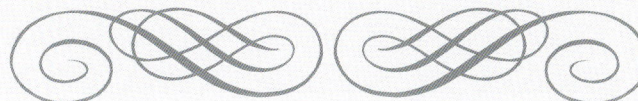

Rest is laying your burdens at the foot of the cross.

Worry is picking them back up again.

Larry says that his sheep simply will not lie down if they are worried or troubled, but when they have confidence in their shepherd, they will be at peace and will lie down—in his presence. The same is true for us, as we choose to trust in our Shepherd's care, and rest in His presence: *"He maketh me lie down in green pastures" (Psalm 23:2).*

In the original language, this verse paints a picture that reveals God's message to us. The Hebrew word for *pasture* means "an abode, a beautiful place to dwell in peace and safety." The words *lie down* mean to "stretch oneself out." This verse portrays a sheep that is so confident in its shepherd that it has no fear. It lies down, stretches out, and becomes vulnerable. It feels safe and secure. It is at peace.

Larry noticed, however, that this peace doesn't come easily for his sheep, and neither does it come easily for us. We are so worried and troubled by the cares of life that we can't lie down and have peace. We'd like to totally trust God, but we sense something fighting within us. Satan prevents us from coming into the peaceful presence of God by burdening us with thoughts of past hurts, worries, and fears for the future, and by distressing us with present troubles and conflicts.

HOW DO YOU FIND PEACE SO YOU CAN LIE DOWN?

Larry told us the answer to lying down in green pastures is found in Philippians 4:6–7: *"Be careful for nothing; but in every thing by prayer and supplication with thanksgiving let your requests be made known unto God. And the peace of God, which passeth all understanding, shall keep your hearts and minds through Christ Jesus."*

The word *careful* means to "be full of worry, troubled with cares, anxious." The word *nothing* means just that, nothing. Do not fear, worry, be troubled, or be anxious about anything. Jesus put it this way: *"Let not your heart be troubled" (John 14:1).* That is not just good counsel—it is a command of the Lord, "Let not . . . ."

> *If we want to have peace, we should simply be at peace.*

Isn't that a strange command? If we want to have peace, we should simply be at peace. This is all the advice the Bible offers. Over and over we read these commands: Do not fear. Be at peace with each other. Do not quarrel. Don't be angry. God is saying that peace is already there, if we want it. We can choose to live in peace, joy, and love, or we can choose to hold on to our bitterness, fears, and conflicts.

God's love is freely given. Through Christ we have access to the presence of God, where we will find the love and peace we so desperately desire. The Kingdom of God is here for us to possess now, if only we'll humble ourselves and choose to lie down in God's green pasture.

DO THOUGHTS OF PAST HURTS BURDEN YOU?

Do you ever rehearse in your mind the offenses others have committed against you? These fiery darts are planted in our minds to prevent us from lying down in green pastures. But when we abide in God's presence, we will find love for those who have hurt us. We will choose love over blaming others and insisting on being right. Instead of being bitter, we will bless them and pray for their well-being. We will be at peace.

DO YOU HAVE FEARS OF THE FUTURE?

Sometimes we may think that a little worry and a little anxiety are indications of how really concerned and spiritual we are, but they actually may indicate how wicked we are. Worrying reveals that we really do not believe that God looks after the practical details of our lives, and therefore worrying is sinful. When we are in the presence of God, we are confident in His power to provide for all our needs and arrange our circumstances. He is our Father and we have nothing to fear. We are at peace.

ARE YOU TROUBLED BY YOUR PRESENT CIRCUMSTANCES?

Our minds become troubled when personal conflicts and afflictions disturb us and cause us to doubt God's love. We become confused and troubled because we don't understand why God is allowing bad things to happen to us, especially when we are trying so hard to be good. When this desire to understand becomes compulsive it can prevent us from entering God's presence and lying down in peace.

If we choose to abide in the presence of God, we won't have to insist on always understanding why things happen or why people act the way they do. Look again at this verse: *". . . The peace of God, which passeth all understanding . . ."* (Philippians 4:7). The word *passeth* is the Greek word *huperecho*, which means "superior to, above, better than." The peace of God is better than understanding. It "surpasses" understanding.

HOW DO WE ENTER GOD'S PRESENCE?

We can't lie down in His pasture unless we lay down the burdens of our past hurts, future fears, and present troubles. Jesus asks us to die to ourselves and cast all our burdens onto His shoulders, thus exchanging them for His light burden.

"Come unto me, all ye that labour and are heavy laden, ... And ye shall find rest unto your souls. For my yoke is easy, and my burden is light" (Matthew 11:28). *"Casting all your care upon him; for he careth for you"* (I Peter 5:7).

As we lay down our burdens and lie down in God's presence, we can stretch out like sheep and become vulnerable. Herein is the mystery of God: through this vulnerability comes strength, for God's power is *"made perfect in weakness"* (II Corinthians 12:9). This reflected peace is proof that we are in God's presence. When we are at peace, God's power can flow through us and we can refuse to be swamped with the cares of this life.

Jesus has already won the victory over our hurts, our fears, and our troubles. Let's forsake all of these burdens so that we can follow our Shepherd into green pastures and lie down. We have nothing to fear.

—Bob

"But thanks be to God, which giveth us the victory through our Lord Jesus Christ. . . . Let not your heart be troubled: neither let it be afraid. . . . Thou shalt lie down, and none shall make thee afraid. . . . And the needy shall lie down in safety . . . . I will feed them in a good pasture, and upon the high mountains of Israel shall their fold be: there shall they lie in a good fold, and in a fat pasture shall they feed upon the mountains of Israel. I will feed my flock, and I will cause them to lie down, saith the Lord GOD. . . . Peace I leave with you, my peace I give unto you. . . . These things I have spoken unto you, that in me ye might have peace. In the world ye shall have tribulation: but be of good cheer; I have overcome the world."

I Corinthians 15:57, John 14:27, Job 11:19, Isaiah 14:30, Ezekiel 34:14–15, John 14:27, John 16:33

CHAPTER THREE

Meditating on
God's Word

Sheep have a complex stomach with multiple chambers. Sheep fill up quickly and then often retire to more secluded spots to bring up what they have swallowed and carefully rechew it. By rechewing their food, sheep get considerably more nourishment out of what they eat.

Such a thing seems pretty gross to us. Just think of it. Chocolate chip cookies are great the first time around, but can you imagine chewing them a second time? It doesn't make sense to us, but it sure makes sense to sheep.

The Psalmist challenges us to meditate on God's Word and "rechew" it, so to speak. This makes God's Word more digestible, more understandable. It makes good sense to chew on God's Word over and over. It makes good sense to meditate.

—Larry

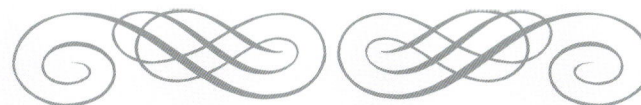

Meditation is the art of asking questions of God.

Impulsiveness is making decisions without God's input.

In the book of Job, God tells Job to *"ask now the beasts, and they shall teach thee; and the fowls of the air, and they shall tell thee: Or speak to the earth, and it shall teach thee: and the fishes of the sea shall declare unto thee. Who knoweth not in all these that the hand of the LORD hath wrought this?" (Job 12:7–9).* In this same manner, Larry observes his sheep ruminating and chewing their cud and then asks us to relate this to the concept of meditation.

HOW DO SHEEP RUMINATE?

> *Meditation is the art of asking questions of God.*

Sheep are even-toed ruminants with four stomachs. They need four stomachs because the leaves, stems, grasses, and weeds that they eat are extremely difficult to digest. Sheep have three forestomachs, which are called the rumen, reticulum, and omasum, and one true stomach, the abomasum. In the first two chambers, the rumen and the reticulum, food mixes with saliva and separates into solid and liquid layers. Solids clump together to form the cud (or bolus). The cud is then regurgitated and chewed slowly to completely mix it with saliva and to break it down into smaller particles. This process gives sheep optimal nutritional value from their food.

Through the act of ruminating, sheep show us how to meditate on God's Word and get spiritual nutrition from it.

The Hebrew word for *meditate* is *siyach*, which means to "study, ponder, reflect on, put forth thoughts, muse, commune, even sing about." When we ponder God's Word throughout the day and commune with God about it, He speaks to us personally, gives us greater insight and understanding, and nourishes our souls with His Spirit.

"When I remember thee upon my bed, and meditate on thee in the night watches . . . I meditate on all thy works; I muse on the work of thy hands . . . I call to remembrance my song in the night: I commune with mine own heart: and my spirit made diligent search . . ." (Psalm 63:6, Psalm 143:5, Psalm 77:6).

God says that we are to hide His Word in our hearts and memorize it, so that we can think about it day and night. When we do that, He promises that we will find reward.

Rumen

Reticulum

Omasum

WHAT REWARDS DOES GOD PROMISE FOR MEDITATING ON HIS WORD?

"This book of the law shall not depart out of thy mouth; but thou shalt meditate therein day and night, that thou mayest observe to do according to all that is written therein: for then thou shalt make thy way prosperous, and then thou shalt have good success . . . But his delight is in the law of the LORD; and in his law doth he meditate day and night . . . and whatsoever he doeth shall prosper . . . When thou goest, it shall lead thee; when thou sleepest, it shall keep thee; and when thou awakest, it shall talk with thee" (Joshua 1:8, Psalm 1:2–3, Proverbs 6:22).

Within the following verses, see if you can identify the special reward for meditating on God's Word: *"Therefore shall ye lay up these my words in your heart and in your soul, and bind them for a sign upon your hand, that they may be as frontlets between your eyes. And ye shall teach them your children, speaking of them when thou sittest in thine house, and when thou walkest by the way, when thou liest down, and when thou risest up. And thou shalt write them upon the door posts of thine house, and upon thy gates: That your days may be multiplied, and the days of your children, in the land which the LORD sware unto your fathers to give them, as the days of heaven upon the earth"* (Deuteronomy 11:18–21).

Did you find it? Isn't this the reward that we all desire: *"days of heaven upon the earth"*? In this verse, the word *heaven* (Hebrew: *shameh*) means "the abode of God." God abides in His Word, and when we meditate on it, we are interacting with God in His abode. Just as sheep lie down in green pastures and ruminate in the presence of their shepherd, so we can lie down in God's abode (the kingdom of heaven) and be in His presence by meditating on His Word. Meditation is coming into God's presence and interacting with Him about His Word.

Meditation is the art of asking questions of God. *"One thing have I desired of the LORD, that will I seek after . . . to enquire in his temple . . . Ask, and it shall be given you . . . For every one that asketh receiveth"* (Psalm 27:4, Matthew 7:7–8). Ask questions like "What does this word mean in its original language?" or "What other verses use this word?" With instant access to online lexicons and study aids, we have unprecedented opportunity to dig into God's Word. As we do so, God will direct us to eternal treasures!

In fact, meditating on God's Word is similar to treasure hunting. Discovering treasure ourselves is far more exciting than looking at treasure someone else has discovered! I've been to the Tower of London and there gazed upon the great Star of Africa diamond, which weighs 530 carats. Gazing into that diamond is like looking into a galaxy. It was cut from the 3,106-carat Cullinan diamond found in South Africa in 1905. As impressed as I was looking at this polished gem, I can only imagine how much more exhilarated Frederick Wells must have been when he dug it out of the earth! And such are the jewels waiting to be discovered in God's Word, if we would only take the time and effort to dig them out, by meditating on God's Word.

WILL YOU SEARCH FOR HIDDEN TREASURES?

Try directing your attention to God's Word, for it is like a treasure map that will guide you to the most precious treasures in the universe. *"Seek, and ye shall find"* (Matthew 7:7). Be like the sheep: ruminate on the Word of God.

—Bob

"Again, the kingdom of heaven is like unto treasure hid in a field . . . If thou seekest her as silver, and searchest for her as for hid treasures; then shalt thou understand the fear of the LORD, and find the knowledge of God . . . In whom [Christ] are hid all the treasures of wisdom and knowledge . . . That I may cause those that love me to inherit substance; and I will fill their treasures . . . the fear of the LORD is his treasure . . . For where your treasure is, there will your heart be also."

Matthew 13:44, Proverbs 2:4–5, Colossians 2:3, Proverbs 8:21, Isaiah 33:6, Matthew 6:21

CHAPTER FOUR

Beside Still Waters

Have you ever walked through heavy morning dew? If you have, you know how much water can collect on blades of grass overnight. As warm moist air cools down below the dew point, water condenses and forms droplets that saturate just about everything.

The Psalmist wrote that the good shepherd leads his sheep beside the quiet water, and the stillest of all water is the early morning dew. Sheep prefer this source of water to all others. For the shepherd to take advantage of still water, he has to rise early and lead his sheep to pasture before the sun dries it up.

For me, the stillest and quietest waters are those early morning moments I've spent with the Lord. Nobody interrupts me and the phone never rings. Try rising early sometime, while the day is still and fresh. Spend that early morning time in God's Word and see how refreshing the quiet waters can be.

—Larry

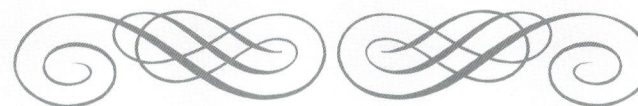

Quietness is emptying your mind of trivia.

Busyness is filling your mind with trivia.

I never thought about the verse *"He leadeth me beside the still waters" (Psalm 23:2)* as referring to the early morning dew, but it makes sense, doesn't it? The early morning dew watered the earth before the Flood: *"But there went up a mist from the earth, and watered the whole face of the ground" (Genesis 2:6).* Just as this dew can quench the thirst of sheep, so the early morning Living Water can satisfy your thirsty soul. The dew is on the grass only in the early morning before the sun dries it away. There is something very special about those quiet, early morning hours in the cool of the day.

In Psalm 23:2, the word *still (menuchah)* means "quiet." The Hebrew word for *waters (mayim)* means "refreshing." The early morning hours offer a refreshing quiet that can't be found at any other time of the day.

WHY DOES GOD ASK US TO SEEK HIM EARLY IN THE MORNING?

God admonishes us to seek Him in the early morning hours (which can also refer to the days of one's youth), because there is a reward for seeking Him early—we'll find Him!

"I love them that love me; and those that seek me early shall find me . . . Remember now thy Creator in the days of thy youth, while the evil days come not, nor the years draw nigh, when thou shalt say, I have no pleasure in them . . . Seek ye the LORD while he may be found, call ye upon him while he is near . . . O God, thou art my God; early will I seek thee: my soul thirsteth for thee, my flesh longeth for thee in a dry and thirsty land, where no water is . . . As the hart panteth after the water brooks, so panteth my soul after thee, O God" (Proverbs 8:17, Ecclesiastes 12:1, Isaiah 55:6, Psalm 63:1, Psalm 42:1).

Notice the strong desire David had to seek after God. Ask yourself, "Do I hunger and thirst after God like that?" If you don't, perhaps you are seeking for it in the wrong place. This desire and energy comes from outside of your self. Perhaps it is like the phenomenon of falling in love.

WHAT IS IT LIKE TO FALL IN LOVE?

Ask your father sometime what it was like when he first fell in love with your mother. When I was courting my wife, I eagerly anticipated being with her. I didn't have to try to work up those feelings—they were there all on their own. She was all I could think about! I wanted to be with her all the time. She could do no wrong. I had fallen in love with her!

I believe God allows people to experience falling in love so they can understand how God loves them. He is deeply in love with every human being He created, and He wants to be with us and interact with us always. He loves us! When we personally experience His intense, unconditional love for us, in spite of our horrible sin, it is absolutely overwhelming! The love of God overflows us so that it flows right back to Him. We then discover that we love Him back with the same intensity and abandon that He has for us! This energy and desire does not come from within ourselves—it radiates from the unconditional love that we absorb from God: *"We love him, because he first loved us" (I John 4:19).*

When we fall into the love of God, we want to interact with Him all the time. One summer, every morning at 5:00 a.m., a bird landed on the railing just outside my bedroom window and loudly began chirping away. When I opened one of my eyes to look, I seemed to hear the bird saying, *"Come away my beloved, come away!" (Song of Solomon 2:10).*

> *The early morning hours offer a time of refreshing quiet that can't be found at any other time of the day.*

Though I was sleepy, I got up and had a sweet time of fellowship with the Lord. I drank of the still, Living Waters while the dew was still on the grass around me. The grass was so wet I had to sit on a cushion! Every morning that summer, the same bird would come to my window at precisely the same time and I would rise up and go outside and have sweet fellowship with the Lord until 7:00 a.m. Then I would go inside, wake the rest of the family, and share with them what I had discovered. What a joy and delight that was!

WHO IN THE BIBLE ROSE EARLY TO SEEK THE LORD?

Let's look and see who rose up early in the morning to seek the Lord.

"And Abraham got up early in the morning to the place where he stood before the LORD" (Genesis 19:27).

"And Moses wrote all the words of the LORD, and rose up early in the morning" (Exodus 24:4).

"And Moses rose up early in the morning, and went up unto Mount Sinai, as the LORD had commanded him" (Exodus 34:4).

"And Joshua rose early in the morning, and the priests took up the ark of the LORD" (Joshua 6:12).

"And . . . [Hannah and Elkanah] rose up in the morning early, and worshipped before the LORD" (I Samuel 1:19).

"And David rose up early in the morning, and left the sheep with a keeper" (I Samuel 17:20).

"And in the morning, rising up a great while before day, . . . [Jesus] went out, and departed into a solitary place, and there prayed" (Mark 1:35).

"And all the people came early in the morning to him in the temple, for to hear him" (Luke 21:38).

"And early in the morning he came again into the temple, and all the people came unto him [Jesus]; and he sat down, and taught them" (John 8:2).

"And when they heard that, they [the apostles] entered into the temple early in the morning, and taught" (Acts 5:21).

"My voice shalt thou hear in the morning, O LORD; in the morning will I direct my prayer unto thee, and will look up" (Psalm 5:3).

"And the first of all the firstfruits of all things [first hours of the day] . . . shall be the priest's: . . . that he may cause the blessing to rest in thine house" (Ezekiel 44:30).

DO YOU WANT A BLESSING IN YOUR HOUSE?

The blessing is being in the presence of God. Do you long to be with God? Then take time to be with Him and give Him the first-fruits of your day. Let Him lead you beside the still waters. Make time to be quiet before the Lord and let Him calm your heart. Let His presence be the blessing that will rest in your house. Are you taking advantage of the early morning hours and drinking from God's still waters?

—Bob

> *"I come to the garden alone,*
> *While the dew is still on the roses*
> *And the voice I hear falling on my ear,*
> *The Son of God discloses.*
> *And He walks with me, and He talks with me,*
> *And He tells me I am His own;*
> *And the joy we share as we tarry there,*
> *None other has ever known."*
>
> C. Austin Miles, 1912

CHAPTER FIVE

Restoring My Soul

Sometimes, when a sheep lies down, it gets a little too comfortable or rolls just a little bit too far one way or the other. Its center of gravity shifts and over it goes.

When this happens, a sheep typically panics and flails its legs wildly in the air. It simply can't get up by itself. It has to lie there till the good shepherd comes to its rescue.

A sheep in this condition is said to be cast. Sometimes we, too, can become cast, cast spiritually. We get too comfortable. We lose our center of balance. We indulge too much one way or the other, and before you know it we're cast like a sheep. We can't get ourselves back on our own two feet without help.

The Psalmist wrote simply, *"He restores my soul."* Aren't you glad that the Good Shepherd is always there? He's always there to restore us when we can't save ourselves.

—Larry

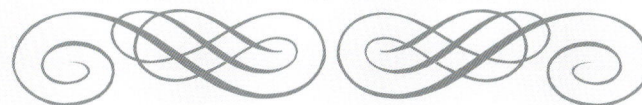

Restoration is looking to God for wisdom and power.

Despair is relying on your own strength.

Larry said that if one of his sheep gets a little too comfortable or indulges a little too much, it can lose its center of balance, roll over on its back, and not be able to get up. In this cast state, a sheep is so uncomfortable that it panics and flails wildly about. It can even become so distressed it can die within a short time, unless it is quickly rolled over and restored to an upright position. Sheep cannot get back up themselves, especially those that are heavily pregnant or are in full wool. Isn't it strange that God would design a creature that is so helpless and so dependent on human beings to rescue it? Perhaps it's an illustration for us: the sheep of God's pasture. And just like sheep, when we become cast down we cannot restore ourselves either.

WHAT DOES IT MEAN TO BE CAST DOWN AND RESTORED?

The Hebrew word for *cast down* is *shachach*, which literally means "to be in despair, to be hopeless." The word *restore* is *shuwb*, which means "to refresh, to be brought back, to return back to God." And so it is with a person's soul.

When we have become cast down and are in despair, we must return back to God's presence. The word *sin* means "to miss the mark, to be separated from God." When we are separated from God, we are in sin and become cast down. The Good Shepherd promises us that He will restore us and bring our souls back into His presence when we cry out to Him. We can't restore ourselves.

David experienced this need to have his soul restored when he wrote in Psalm 42: *"Why art thou cast down, O my soul? and why art thou disquieted in me?"* This was a conversation that David's spirit was having with his soul. Our soul and our spirit talk to each other throughout the day. It happens to be the most important conversation that we will have.

HOW DOES OUR SOUL BECOME CAST DOWN?

The soul (Hebrew: *nephesh*) consists of three areas:
1. The mind (what you think about)
2. The appetite (the will and what you desire)
3. The seat of the emotions (your affections and passions)

Here is where our battles take place. Satan will attack us in these three areas and do whatever he can to cast us down so we will leave God's presence and the peace, joy, and love that we have there with Him.

The mind battles with thoughts that are not true. Satan may persuade us to think that God is no longer in control or that God doesn't love us any more because of something we have done. Satan puts in our minds disturbing thoughts that convince us that we are all alone and that all is lost. He wants us to believe that he is more powerful than God.

The will battles with despair when we fail. Satan tries to persuade us to give up our will to fight the good fight of faith. When we fail, he knocks us down. He wants us to be so discouraged that we stay down, give up hope, and remain in despair.

Satan also attacks our emotions with his fiery darts. He causes us to remember the hurtful things people have done to us in the past. He reopens these wounds so

> *Come and return to Jesus and let Him restore your soul.*

they can't heal. We become tormented with these fiery darts. If Satan can't get us to bring our past hurts and bitterness into the present moment, then he will try to get us to fear the future and all of its uncertainties. These fears and hurts can quickly overpower us, causing our souls to be cast down.

If we entertain Satan's lies and are persuaded to leave the peace, love, and joy of being in the presence of God, we soon become overwhelmed with fear and hurt. We may become so depressed that we no longer have any desire to try to get up. Like sheep in this state, we are truly cast down and cannot get up by ourselves. We need to seek comfort.

WHERE DO PEOPLE GO TO FIND COMFORT?

When we are cast down, we often seek comfort from our friends. We want someone to come alongside, comfort, and sympathize with us. We want the attention of someone who understands our pain and feels our hurt. Unfortunately, this kind of sympathy may feel good, but it doesn't help us get up. Though it may be comforting for the moment, it does not restore us.

Many people attempt to find comfort in financial security, healthy lifestyles, worldly possessions, and influential positions. All these provide a measure of temporary comfort, but only the Good Shepherd can restore us. Take a moment to consider other forms of comfort that people often seek.

HOW DOES OUR GOOD SHEPHERD COMFORT US?

When we cry out to our Good Shepherd for help, we find true comfort. The Greek word for *comfort* is *parakaleo*. It means to "admonish, strengthen, and encourage." This word is wonderfully illustrated in the Bayeux Tapestry of 1077 A.D., which depicts the history of England. A frame in this tapestry is titled "Bishop Odo Comforting His Troops." In this frame, Bishop Odo is shown "comforting" his troops into battle by goading them from behind with a long, sharp stick and encouraging them to enter into the fight. This may not appear to our modern minds as being comforting, but it reveals a powerful picture of what Paul meant when he spoke of God's comfort: *"Who comforteth us in all our tribulation"* (II Corinthians 1:4).

God's comfort restores our soul. He doesn't allow us to wallow in self-pity or to be content with the empathy of friends. He reminds us that the battle has already been won, and He prods us to get up. However, God's comfort is complete. He prods us, but He also lifts us up when we do not have the strength to save ourselves.

Consider God's complete comfort, which includes both prodding and lifting: *"In the name of Jesus Christ of Nazareth rise up and walk . . . Fight the good fight of faith . . . Above all, taking the shield of faith, wherewith ye shall be able to quench all the fiery darts of the wicked . . . Humble yourselves in the sight of the Lord, and he shall lift you up"* (Acts 3:6, I Timothy 6:12, Ephesians 6:16, James 4:10).

Are you weary today? Are you heavy-hearted? Do you need your soul restored? Then abandon your hurts, your fears, and your anxieties, which only cast you down. Respond to Jesus' gentle prodding. Let Him lift you up—only then will you discover the fullness of His joy.

—Bob

> *"Though he fall, he shall not be utterly cast down: for the LORD upholdeth him with his hand . . . When men are cast down, then thou shalt say, There is lifting up; and he shall save the humble person . . . Humble yourselves in the sight of the Lord, and he shall lift you up . . . Restore unto me the joy of thy salvation; and uphold me with thy free spirit . . . Now thanks be unto God, which always causeth us to triumph in Christ."*
>
> *Psalm 37:24, Job 22:29, James 4:10, Psalm 51:12, II Corinthians 2:14*

CHAPTER SIX

Paths of Righteousness

Recently, I was reflecting on how our sheep follow me willingly as I lead them to fresh pasture each day. I thought of Jesus' words: *"My sheep hear my voice, and I know them, and they follow me."* It was really cool! I began to think of myself as a good shepherd.

It wasn't long before I found several sheep outside the fence. I called, but they ignored my voice. They willingly followed when I led them somewhere they wanted to go, but if not, they stubbornly refused to follow.

As I watched those sheep, I realized that sometimes our response to God's leading is also conditional. We follow when He leads us where we want to go, but we ignore His voice when we set our mind on other pastures. Sometimes we need to be reminded that true obedience requires us to yield to His voice wherever, whenever, and whatever.

—Larry

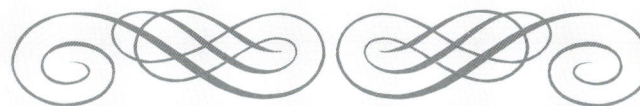

Obedience is staying close to your Shepherd.

Willfulness is choosing to go your own way.

Larry discovered that when a shepherd leads his sheep where they want to go, they willingly follow him. But when the shepherd leads them somewhere they don't want to go, they stubbornly refuse to follow. We are just like those sheep. We tend to follow Jesus when He leads us to green pastures and places we want to go. However, when the Path of Righteousness leads us to places where we don't want to go, we tend to wander away from our Shepherd.

WHAT IS TRUE OBEDIENCE?

Our willingness to obey Jesus may be likened to children who eagerly obey their father when he tells them to eat a bowl of their favorite ice cream. It's easy to obey a command when you already want to do it. But the true test of obedience is to obey even when you don't want to—when it may not be enjoyable, convenient, or desirable for you. Like Larry says, "True obedience means we yield to His voice wherever, whenever, and whatever."

Satan tries to persuade us to wander off the Path of Righteousness by telling us that we don't have to obey God—that we will be happier doing what we want to do. Isn't this what Satan told Eve when he whispered into her ear, *"Hath God said?" (Genesis 3:1).* Eve listened to his voice and tragically followed it right out of the Garden into despair and regret.

Satan also tried to persuade Jesus in the wilderness. He even used God's Word to try to convince Jesus to leap off the pinnacle of the temple (Luke 4:9–11). Jesus heard His Father's words, but knowing it was not His Father's voice, He resisted Satan's temptation. True obedience to God requires us to first distinguish His voice from all others.

CAN YOU DISCERN GOD'S VOICE?

Notice what this verse says: *"My sheep hear my voice and they follow" (John 10:27).* It doesn't say that God's sheep hear His *words* and follow but that they hear His *voice*. The danger is that voices can sound very similar, and Satan is able to imitate God's voice quite well. He will even use God's own words and twist them, trying to trick us into following him. Satan deceives us into doing what he wants us to do by making us think that we are following God.

This is illustrated in Matthew 16:15–23, when Jesus asked His disciples who they thought He was. Peter answered, *"Thou art the Christ, the Son of the living God."* Jesus explained to Peter that God had put that thought

in his mind: *"Flesh and blood hath not revealed it unto thee, but my Father which is in heaven."* Just four verses later, Jesus told His disciples that He must go to Jerusalem and be killed. This time Peter rebuked Jesus and said, *"Lord: this shall not be unto thee."* Jesus responded, *"Get thee behind me, Satan."* He was showing Peter that Satan had put that thought in his mind. Like Peter, we need to learn to distinguish God's voice from Satan's.

> *The true test of obedience is obeying when you don't want to.*

HOW CAN YOU BE SURE YOU'RE FOLLOWING GOD'S VOICE?

Notice what Jesus says will happen to people in the last days: *"And Jesus answered and said unto them, Take heed that no man deceive you. For many shall come in my name, saying, I am Christ; and shall deceive many"* (Matthew 24:4–5). If deceived people don't know they are deceived and actually believe that they are following the Truth, how can we be sure we are following Jesus and not an impostor?

We need to recognize God's voice. A little child recognizes his father's voice in a crowd of people because he has heard it his entire life. Since father and son have spent hours talking, the little child can distinguish his father's voice, even though other voices may sound similar.

Science tells us that the human voice is actually more unique than a person's fingerprints. No two voices sound exactly the same. This is also true of spiritual voices. A child of God will hear his heavenly Father's voice, it will resonate with him, and he will be able to distinguish it from other voices pretending to be God's.

God's voice is very still. In order for His sheep to hear it, we must stop talking, be quiet, and listen carefully. Our Shepherd's voice is loving, humble, compassionate, and forgiving. The butcher's voice is harsh, proud, critical, and condemning. Our own voices may be selfish, arrogant, lazy, and judgmental. It's important for us to listen to the right voice. Only the Shepherd's voice leads us on the Path of Righteousness.

WHERE DOES THE PATH LEAD US?

If we follow the Good Shepherd on the Path of Righteousness, we will soon discover that our destination is a deeper relationship with God.

God is not a bachelor—He wants to have a relationship with us. He's looking for a Bride to rejoice over *". . . As the bridegroom rejoiceth over the bride, so shall thy God rejoice over thee"* (Isaiah 62:5). When we understand His amazing love toward us, we will say, "I do" to His invitation. Then we will follow Him wherever He goes, simply because we want to be with Him.

What if the Path of Righteousness looks frightening and difficult or it just doesn't make sense? Will you leave the Good Shepherd and wander away? You won't if He is your First Love. However, if you wander away from Him and choose your own path, you will no longer hear the voice of your Beloved saying, *"Arise, my love, my fair one, and come away!"* (Song of Solomon 2:13).

Do you hear the Good Shepherd's voice beckoning you to follow Him on the Path of Righteousness? Will you listen whenever He speaks, obey whatever He says, and follow Him wherever He goes? *"Then Jesus beholding him loved him, and said . . . come, take up the cross, and follow me"* (Mark 10:21).

—Bob

> *"Cause me to know the way wherein I should walk; for I lift up my soul unto thee . . . And thine ears shall hear a word behind thee, saying, This is the way, walk ye in it . . . And a highway shall be there, and a way, and it shall be called The way of holiness . . . I will instruct thee and teach thee in the way which thou shalt go: I will guide thee with mine eye . . . I will lead them in paths that they have not known: I will make darkness light before them."*
>
> *Psalm 143:8, Isaiah 30:21, Isaiah 35:8, Psalm 32:8, Isaiah 42:16*

CHAPTER SEVEN

Through the Valley

When David said, *"Yea though I walk through the valley of the shadow,"* he may have been on his way to the high pastures. We know that in the heat of summer, grass dries up and withers in the lower pastures. However, grasses in the high pastures are in their prime because rains and heavy dew still water them daily.

To get his sheep to the high pastures, a shepherd had to lead them through the valleys and along tight, winding trails covered with dark shadows. It was rough going, but the trials were worth it. There was plenty to eat in the high pastures.

Our Good Shepherd may also lead us through some long and dark valleys, but it is comforting to know where He's headed. He is leading us to the high pastures, where the grass is still green and the waters are quiet. The valleys may seem difficult, but they are worth it in the end when we come out on the other side.

—Larry

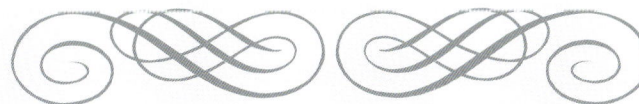

Endurance is refusing to quit till the journey is over.

Weariness is allowing shadows to wear you down.

The Path of Righteousness brought David to the entrance of the valley of the shadow of death: *"Yea, though I walk through the valley of the shadow of death, I will fear no evil" (Psalm 23:4).* Larry said that the sheep do not know that the pathway through the dark, narrow, foreboding valley will eventually lead them to the high pastures, where there is an abundance of grass and water. Neither would they know that the shepherd had already passed through the valley on his way to the high plateau. There he would have prepared a "table" for the sheep (a pasture in the high plateau) by pulling out the thistles and poisonous weeds. Then he would have gone back down to the dry plain to get his flock before leading them to the high pasture. The sheep would be fearful of entering the valley of the shadow of death. The Good Shepherd tells the sheep of His pasture to "fear no evil."

> *We can discover Christ in the valley in ways we could never find Him on the plain.*

WHY SHOULD WE NOT FEAR LEAVING THE COMFORT OF THE LOWER PASTURES?

In the Song of Solomon, Jesus describes Himself, saying, *"I am the rose of Sharon, and the lily of the valleys" (Song of Solomon 2:1).* This little verse gives great insight into why our Shepherd leads us out of comfortable pastures and into the Valley of the Shadow.

First, the word *Sharon* means "a plain." It's a word picture depicting a flat, level, sunny plain where one can see a long way. Christ describes Himself as the Rose on this plain. This is a picture of life when it is good. We can see a long distance. The sky is clear and the sun is warm. The road is easy, flat, and comfortable. There is no fear, and there are no surprises. Life is predictable and full of splendor and majesty. These are the times when life is pleasant, and we can stop along the path and take the time to admire the beauty of the Rose of Sharon.

". . . The desert shall rejoice, and blossom as the rose. It shall blossom abundantly, and rejoice even with joy and singing: the glory of Lebanon shall be given unto it, the excellency of Carmel and Sharon, they shall see the glory of the LORD, and the excellency of our God . . . And Sharon shall be a fold of flocks, and the valley of Achor a place for the herds to lie down in, for my people that have sought me" (Isaiah 35:1–2, Isaiah 65:10).

WHAT IS DISCOVERED IN THE VALLEY OF THE SHADOW?

Christ also describes Himself as "the lily of the valleys." Lilies are grown in the shadows. The valley is dark, confining, and frightening. We don't know where the path may lead or what we may encounter around the next bend. There are potential dangers on every side. The path is steep, rough, and difficult. The first thing we want to do upon entering the valley is to get out as quickly as possible. We don't like it there, and we'd rather be back on the sunny plain. But our Shepherd leads us through this valley for a reason only He knows.

The Shepherd has a special purpose for our being in this valley. He wants us to trust Him there. Instead of frantically looking for a way out, He wants us to search for the beautiful, fragrant, lily of the valley growing there. The lily of the valley has small, bell-shaped petals, and its fragrance is absolutely delightful! This tiny flower represents the tender beauty of Christ found through suffering.

intimacy." The word *sufferings* means "calamity, evil, or the afflictions which Christians must undergo in behalf of the same cause which Christ patiently endured." Only in the valley of the shadow of death can we understand what it means to partake in the sweet fellowship of the sufferings of Christ.

Are you in the valley right now? Seek diligently for the Lily of the Valley. Once you have found Christ through suffering, you will experience an intimacy with Him that cannot be obtained any other way.

—Bob

WHY IS THE VALLEY CALLED THE SHADOW OF DEATH?

The word *death* means "despair, darkness, or extreme danger." Jesus walked through this valley many times. If we are going to follow in His steps, then we can know the path will inevitably lead us to this valley. It's called "death" because we have to die to our own desires and selves if we are going to follow our Good Shepherd through it. In this valley of despair, darkness, danger, and death, we can discover Christ in a way that we never could on the plain. Here in the valley, we can identify with His sufferings:

"Surely he hath borne our griefs, and carried our sorrows: yet we did esteem him stricken, smitten of God, and afflicted . . . From that time forth began Jesus to show unto his disciples, how that he must go unto Jerusalem, and suffer many things of the elders and chief priests and scribes . . . But those things, which God before had showed by the mouth of all his prophets, that Christ should suffer, he hath so fulfilled . . . For Christ also hath once suffered for sins, the just for the unjust, that he might bring us to God" (Isaiah 53:4, Matthew 16:21, Acts 3:18, I Peter 3:18).

HAVE YOU EXPERIENCED THE FELLOWSHIP OF CHRIST'S SUFFERINGS?

"That I may know him, and the power of his resurrection, and the fellowship of his sufferings . . ." (Philippians 3:10). The word *fellowship* means "interaction or

> "*. . . Because Christ also suffered for us, leaving us an example, that ye should follow his steps . . . For unto you it is given in the behalf of Christ, not only to believe on him, but also to suffer for his sake . . . Forasmuch then as Christ hath suffered for us in the flesh, arm yourselves likewise with the same mind: for he that hath suffered in the flesh hath ceased from sin . . . If we suffer, we shall also reign with him: if we deny him, he also will deny us . . . Yea, and all that will live godly in Christ Jesus shall suffer persecution . . . And they departed from the presence of the council, rejoicing that they were counted worthy to suffer shame for his name . . . we told you before that we should suffer tribulation . . . But, if, when ye do well, and suffer for it, ye take it patiently, this is acceptable with God . . . if ye suffer for righteousness' sake, happy are ye: and be not afraid of their terror, neither be troubled . . . For it became him . . . to make the captain of their salvation perfect through sufferings.*"

> *I Peter 2:21, Philippians 1:29, I Peter 4:1, II Timothy 2:12, II Timothy 3:12, Acts 5:41, I Thessalonians 3:4, I Peter 2:20, I Peter 3:17,14, Hebrews 2:10*

CHAPTER EIGHT

Thy Rod and Staff

I can remember falling off my bicycle while attempting some foolish tricks as a kid. I still wear the scars, but the thing I remember most was how my mom and dad comforted me. As they lovingly wiped away my tears, they also laid down a few new rules.

The Psalmist wrote, *"Your rod and your staff comfort me."* A good shepherd carried both. The rod represented his power and authority. The staff was a symbol of his compassion and kindness.

As parents, we, too, need to comfort our children with both a rod and a staff. The rod sets boundaries and corrects while the staff gently guides and restores. The rod without the staff leads to harshness. The staff without the rod leads to permissiveness. Remember the words of the Psalmist and carry both a rod and a staff when you comfort your children.

—Larry

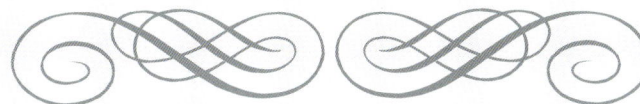

Comfort is applying rules with gentleness and consistency.

Abuse is stepping outside the limits of your authority.

In this short devotional, Larry not only explains the difference between a shepherd's rod and staff, but he also explains why a good shepherd needs both of them, not just one or the other.

In Zechariah 11:7, a shepherd is described as having two "staves" (Hebrew: *makkale*), which can mean either a rod or a staff. The shepherd gives names to these staves to identify their distinct uses. He calls the rod "Bands," and he calls the staff "Beauty": *"I took unto me two staves; the one I called Beauty, and the other I called Bands; and I fed the flock."* These names reaffirm the different uses of a rod and a staff, which are both used to help direct the flock.

WHAT IS THE PURPOSE OF THE SHEPHERD'S ROD?

The word *rod* (Hebrew: *shebet*) found in Psalm 23:4 means "scepter, club, or authority." It suggests the same use as the rod called "Bands" in Zechariah. The word used for *Bands* means "to writhe, twist, travail, ruin or break." While this may seem to be an appropriate use of a rod against enemies, the shepherd also used the rod against sheep that resisted his authority. The pain inflicted upon a lamb was preferable to the possible destruction that awaited it if it strayed away from the watchful eye of the shepherd: *"And they became meat to all the beasts of the field, when they were scattered"* (Ezekiel 34:5).

Perhaps you've heard the story of the shepherd who used his rod to break the leg of the wandering lamb who would not stay near him. There is some debate as to whether or not shepherds ever did this, but the principle of chastening is scriptural. After breaking the lamb's leg, the shepherd would have had to carry the lamb everywhere he went while it healed. This would create such a bond between the two of them that when the lamb's leg finally healed and it could walk, it would never stray from the shepherd's side again. The shepherd knew how to use the rod effectively, and he had the authority to use it when the lamb needed it.

The Lord disciplines His children in much the same way: *"My son, despise not the chastening of the LORD; neither be weary of his correction . . . If ye endure chastening, God dealeth with you as with sons; for what son is he whom the father chasteneth not? . . . Now no chastening for the present seemeth to be joyous, but grievous: nevertheless afterward it yieldeth the peaceable fruit of righteousness unto them which are exercised thereby"* (Proverbs 3:11; Hebrews 12:7, 11).

> *A good parent will use both the rod and the staff, not just one or the other.*

WHAT IS THE PURPOSE OF THE SHEPHERD'S STAFF?

In Psalm 23:4, the word *staff* (Hebrew: *mishenah*) means "support of any kind, to lean on." It comes from the Hebrew word *shawan*, which means "to lean upon, to trust in God." It illustrates resting on the Lord and leaning on the Lord's staff rather than using one's own strength to accomplish God's work. The shepherd in the book of Zechariah called his staff "Beauty," which means "kindness, pleasant, delightful." The shepherd's staff was used with kindness on the sheep, and he would even gently stroke and pet the sheep with it. It was indeed pleasant and beautiful to the little lamb to be comforted by the staff while walking beside the shepherd.

HOW ARE PARENTS TO USE THE ROD AND STAFF?

Just as the Lord chastens us and has compassion on us, we should also model that behavior while training our children. Good parents will use both the rod and staff in training their children, not just one or the other. As Larry said, the parent who uses the rod of discipline without the staff of kindness and compassion becomes harsh and angry, and his children will fear him. The parent who uses the staff of kindness without the rod of discipline will become permissive, and his children will not respect him nor will they listen to him.

HOW DOES USE OF THE ROD AND STAFF EXPLAIN BALANCING TRUTHS?

The shepherd's use of both the rod and staff illustrates an important concept of truth. Truth in Scripture is usually balanced by a contrasting principle. At first glance, this contrasting principle may seem to contradict the truth, but deeper study reveals that it prevents the truth from being misunderstood. For instance, the shepherd is supposed to be strong and authoritarian, but he is also supposed to be supportive and merciful. Which one is true? Both are true! One without the other leads to imbalance. One without the other leads to a misuse of authority. One without the other does not apply God's whole truth. *"What will ye? Shall I come unto you with a rod, or in love, and in the spirit of meekness?" (I Corinthians 4:21).* The shepherd carries both a rod and staff in order to balance the truth and uses whichever is needful at the time.

WHAT ARE OTHER EXAMPLES OF BALANCING TRUTHS?

Is God a God of love and mercy, or is He a God of justice who punishes the wicked every day? Does man have a free will and make his own choices, or does a sovereign God make all of the choices for him? Is man made in the image of God, or is man's heart desperately wicked and no good thing can come from it? Is man under grace or law?

These and other seemingly paradoxical truths in Scripture describe infinite concepts that cannot be resolved in our tiny, finite brains. We must simply humble ourselves and admit we're unable to intellectually resolve these paradoxes. We must agree with God that both are true.

WHERE DO WE FIND TRUTH?

We'll never be able to completely understand God. He cannot be reduced to mechanical formulas. God is relational and He wants us to interact with Him simply and personally. There, in the presence of our God, we experience the rod and staff of Truth—Jesus Christ: *"I am the way, the truth, and the life: no man cometh unto the Father, but by me . . . Come unto me" (John 14:6, Matthew 11:28).*

—Bob

> *"He hath sent me to bind up the brokenhearted . . . And Jesus, when he came out, saw much people, and was moved with compassion toward them, because they were as sheep not having a shepherd . . . God anointed Jesus of Nazareth with the Holy Ghost and with power: who went about doing good, and healing all that were oppressed of the devil; for God was with him . . . He healeth the broken in heart, and bindeth up their wounds . . . Cause me to know the way wherein I should walk . . . lead me into the land of uprightness."*
>
> Isaiah 61:1, Mark 6:34, Acts 10:38, Psalm 147:3, Psalm 143:8, 10

CHAPTER NINE

Preparing a Table

When the Psalmist wrote, *"You prepare a table before me,"* he may have been referring to a high flat plateau called a mesa. A mesa is a high, flat plain where the pastures flourish in the summer. A shepherd would lead his sheep through the valleys in order to find these "tables" of good grass. However, he always visited the high pastures before he ever took his sheep there.

He made the long and arduous trip alone—with just his rod and staff for comfort. The purpose of his early visit was to prepare the pasture for his sheep. He had to remove poisonous weeds, thistles, and burrs from the table. Most importantly, he had to boldly face the wolves and other predators that claimed these high pastures for themselves. Before he could lead his sheep to the table, he had to make sure it was safe.

Aren't you glad your Good Shepherd goes before you and prepares your table?

—Larry

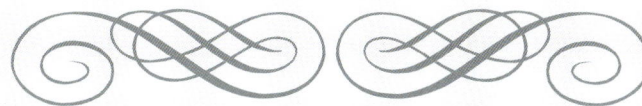

Security is trusting the Shepherd to make your "table" safe.

Fear is being distracted by your enemies.

Larry reminds us that our Good Shepherd is preparing *"a table before . . . [us] in the presence of . . . [our] enemies" (Psalm 23:5)*. We can receive wonderful insight by looking into the meanings of key words in this verse and related passages.

HOW DOES THE LORD PREPARE A TABLE FOR US?

Larry used the metaphor of the table as being a high plateau. He told us that the shepherd went to it before he led his sheep there. The word *preparest* (Hebrew: *arak*) means "to set in a row, put in order." Planting in rows was suitable for the valley but not the high country. The shepherd did not usually plant crops in rows for the sheep or build orderly fences on the plateau. Instead, he often walked for days on end searching for natural grasses, natural sources of water, and natural shelters.

He slept on hard rocks and endured cold nights in order to prepare a place for his sheep. He removed the thistles, burrs, and the poisonous plants. He faced the predators that lurked in the caves of these high places. And he did it all alone with only his rod and staff.

Our Good Shepherd also endured hardship in order to prepare a place for us. In John 14:2–3 Jesus said: *"I go to prepare a place for you. And if I go and prepare a place for you, I will come again, and receive you unto myself; that where I am, there ye may be also."* He walked mile after mile across the regions of the Galilee, endured the cold rejection of men, and faced the wickedness of His enemies. And He did it all alone.

When we look up the word *table* in Hebrew, we discover another definition that gives even further application for our lives. A table (*sulchan*) means "a king's table with sacred uses." Imagine that our Good Shepherd, the King of Kings, the Almighty Creator of heaven and earth, has personally furnished a banquet table for us in the presence of our enemies. He invites us to sit down with Him, eat with Him, and enjoy His presence forever and ever: *"I will come in to him, and will sup with him, and he with me" (Revelation 3:20)*.

DO YOUR ENEMIES STILL CAUSE YOU TO FEAR?

Your enemies (Hebrew: *tsarar*) are "those who cause you distress, harass you, show hostility towards you." When you have enemies who have offended you and never made it right, it is very difficult to sit at the Lord's table and commune with your Shepherd. Instead of focusing on the Lord, your mind wanders to your enemies, you become distressed by how they hurt you, and you want them to experience the pain they caused you.

> *You have nothing to fear as long as you are sitting at the table of the King.*

If that describes you, then you have yet to reach the high pasture. You're still in the valley of fear and death. You haven't died to yourself nor have you blessed those who have cursed you. When you discover the Lily of the Valley, you will love your enemies. They will no longer cause you distress—you will have peace. You will no longer seek for revenge or justice. Then you will be in the high pasture at the King's table, and you will sup with Him in the presence of your enemies.

HOW DID ESTHER BEHAVE IN THE PRESENCE OF HER ENEMY?

The story of Esther (Esther 7) illustrates what it means to sit at the king's table in the presence of your enemies. Esther did not fear her archenemy, Haman, even though he sat at the table with her and had plotted to kill both Esther and her people. Esther placed her confidence in her king, knowing that her enemy Haman had no power over her as long as she was with her king. Perhaps this great example of trust grew out of Esther's previous experience of walking through dark valleys. Remember that Esther lost her parents at an early age, but God led her through that dark valley into the adoptive arms of her uncle, Mordecai.

Do you display the peace and confidence of Esther? Are you able to sit down at the table the Lord has prepared for you? Can you sup with Him even if your enemies sit at the same table? Esther knew that she didn't have to take matters into her own hands. She didn't have to defend herself against her enemy. It was the king's responsibility to defend her, and she trusted her king.

"Therefore if thou bring thy gift to the altar, and there rememberest that thy brother hath ought against thee; leave there thy gift before the altar, and go thy way; first be reconciled to thy brother, and then come and offer thy gift . . . But let a man examine himself, and so let him eat of that bread, and drink of that cup. For he that eateth and drinketh unworthily, eateth and drinketh damnation to himself, not discerning the Lord's body. For this cause many are weak and sickly among you, and many sleep" (Matthew 5:23–24, I Corinthians 11: 28–30).

Christ has prepared the table in this high plateau by giving His own body and blood to be the bread and wine: *"The cup of blessing which we bless, is it not the communion of the blood of Christ? The bread which we break, is it not the communion of the body of Christ"* (I Corinthians 10:16).

Are you at peace with your enemies? You have nothing to fear while you are sitting at the table of the King: *"Abide thou with me, fear not: for he that seeketh my life seeketh thy life: but with me thou shalt be in safeguard"* (I Samuel 22:23).

—Bob

WHAT ARE THE SACRED USES OF THE KING'S TABLE?

The table our Shepherd has prepared for us is "a king's table with sacred uses." He has removed all the poisonous weeds of bitterness that multiplied like thistles and stuck to us like burrs. Now free of them, we can commune with God and with one another. This is the Lord's communion table. Before we come to this table, we are told to examine our relationship with God and with each other. We are warned not to partake of the communion supper unless we can demonstrate the love of Christ to one another by confessing our sins and forgiving one another.

"Can God furnish a table in the wilderness . . . Come eat of my bread and drink of the wine which I have mingled . . . Whoso eateth my flesh, and drinketh my blood, hath eternal life; and I will raise him up at the last day . . . He that eateth my flesh, and drinketh my blood, dwelleth in me, and I in him . . . hearken diligently unto me, and eat ye that which is good, and let your soul delight itself in fatness."

Psalm 78:19; Proverbs 9:5; John 6:54, 56; Isaiah 55:2

CHAPTER TEN

Anointing My Head

Summertime is fly time. And with flies come irritation and torment for sheep. You really don't want to know the details. It is enough to know that sheep will beat their heads against trees or rocks in panicked attempts to end the torture.

But the good shepherd anoints his sheep with oil. The old-fashioned recipes called for some linseed oil, some sulfur, and a little tar. The good shepherd would spread the concoction on the head of each sheep. The oil didn't eliminate the flies, but it kept the flies from landing.

We, too, can experience irritations that come at us like flies. No single problem may be all that bad, but when the irritations start to swarm, it's sometimes overwhelming. Remember the words of the Psalmist. Let the Good Shepherd anoint your head with His oil. The flies may keep buzzing, but they won't be able to touch you.

—Larry

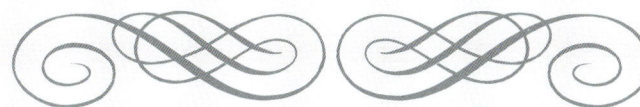

Peace is receiving God's gift of protection.

Irritation is allowing the "flies" of this world to touch you.

We continue the previous devotional, still at the table that the Lord has prepared for us. We are at the communion table of the Lord, having sweet fellowship with our Shepherd and with one another. Something else takes place at this table that is quite significant: *"Thou anointest my head with oil"* (Psalm 23:5).

The Hebrew word for *anoint* (*dashen*) literally means "to be made fat, to become prosperous," and it has two Biblical applications. It can refer to the common practice of applying medicinal ointment to treat ailments, so that an animal can become fat and healthy, or it can indicate a sacred anointing so that one can become prosperous in God's service.

WHY ARE SHEEP ANOINTED WITH OIL?

The shepherd anoints his sheep with a mixture of linseed oil, sulfur, and tar. Larry explained that the purpose of the oil is to repel irritating flies that torment the sheep so that the sheep will be able to feed without distraction and become fat and healthy.

The linseed oil is derived from flax seed, which has medicinal qualities. Mixed with sulfur and tar, it deters flies from landing on the face of the sheep and then crawling up the sheep's nostrils to lay their eggs inside the sinus cavities of the sheep's head.

This is a graphic illustration of how our ever-present enemy tempts us to fear, to doubt, to worry, and to relive past offenses and hurts, even after we have forgiven those who have offended us. Satan's "flies" can enter our minds, lay their eggs, multiply, and overwhelm our thoughts and imagination. Then we begin to rehearse these offenses and emotionally relive them over and over.

These molesting thoughts not only distract us from living in harmony with one another but also prevent us from being in the presence of God and feeding on His Word. Unless we are regularly anointed with the oil of Christ's love, demonstrated through communion, these "flies" in our head will torment us, just like those flies torment the sheep.

At the communion table, our Good Shepherd anoints our head with the oil of the Holy Spirit. This is the "balm of Gilead" that soothes irritations caused by those thoughts that recur, irritate, and torment us. Only when we are in God's presence are we able to gird up the loins of our minds and take captive every thought to the obedience of Christ. Then the healing balm of Christ will restore unto us the same thoughts of peace, love, and mercy that Christ had toward His enemies. Then, like Larry's sheep, we can eat without distraction, and our souls will grow fat and prosper.

"Is there no balm in Gilead; is there no physician there? . . . [Love] shall cover the multitude of sins. . . . We know that we have passed from death unto life, because we love the brethren. . . . Wherefore gird up the loins of your mind . . . . Casting down imaginations, and every high thing that exalteth itself against the knowledge of God, and bringing into captivity every thought to the obedience of Christ. . . . And the LORD shall guide thee continually, and satisfy thy soul in drought, and make fat thy bones: and thou shalt be like a watered garden. . . . I will feed them in a good pasture, and upon the high mountains of Israel shall their fold be: there shall they lie in a good fold, and in a fat pasture shall they feed upon the mountains of Israel" (Jeremiah 8:22, I Peter 4:8, I John 3:14, I Peter 1:13, II Corinthians 10:5, Isaiah 58:11, Ezekiel 34:14).

WHY ARE PEOPLE ANOINTED WITH OIL?

The word *anoint* can also refer to the act of being consecrated to God so one can become prosperous in His service. This anointing is also done with oil. The Hebrew word for *oil*, *shemen*, means "fatness, fruitful land, olive oil."

The process of anointing uses oil liberally as a symbol of the fullness of God's blessing that comes through unity. This was illustrated when Aaron was anointed to be the first high priest: *"Behold how good and how pleasant it is for the brethren to dwell together in unity. It is like the precious ointment upon the head, that ran down upon the beard, even Aaron's beard: that went down to the skirts of his garments; as the dew of Hermon, and as the dew that descended upon the mountains of Zion: for there the LORD commanded the blessing, even life for evermore"* (Psalm 133).

In the New Testament the extravagant fullness of God's blessing is illustrated in this verse: *"And of his fulness have all we received, and grace for grace" (John 1:16)*. The Greek word for *fullness* is *pleroma*, and it uses an illustration of "a ship that has been filled." The Greek lexicon explains that this ship can be filled with sailors, rowers, and soldiers, and it can also be filled with the riches of God, the power of God, and the presence of God.

> *This is the "balm of Gilead" that soothes irritations caused by tormenting thoughts.*

When we are anointed with oil for God's service, this ship is sent to us from God, overflowing with the gifts of the fullness of God's riches, power, and presence, and it is sailing straight to our harbor. We are to bring our little cart to this harbor, where the entire cargo is loaded onto our cart with overflowing abundance. We cannot possibly receive it all, and it spills over and blesses everyone we come in contact with! We receive the riches of God's grace, so we can give His grace to others as it spills out of us and overflows. We don't even have to try.

HOW DOES ONE BECOME ANOINTED WITH THIS ABUNDANT FULLNESS?

The answer is found hidden in the process by which oil is extracted from olives. The Greek word for *oil press* is *gethsemane*. When olives are placed under tremendous pressure, the olive oil that is released is reddish brown in color, almost identical to the color of human blood. This unrefined oil reminds us of the great drops of blood that Jesus sweat when he was praying in Gethsemane: *". . . And his sweat was as it were great drops of blood falling down to the ground" (Luke 22:44)*. It was here, in the oil press of Gethsemane, where the suffering Christ willingly died to His own desires and surrendered to the will of His Father, and out of Christ flowed the abundant grace of God: *"Father, if thou be willing, remove this cup from me: nevertheless, not my will but Thine be done" (Luke 22:42)*.

With this grace, Jesus received the joyful desire and the power to go to the cross and die for us all: *". . . Who for the joy that was set before him endured the cross, despising the shame, and is set down at the right hand of the throne of God" (Hebrews 12:2)*. Now we can follow Christ's example and allow the oil press

of suffering to squeeze out of us the sacred oil of the abundant grace of God. With this grace we can receive from our "ship in the harbor" the fullness of the riches and the presence of God and the overflowing power of the Holy Spirit that will enable us to do God's will.

Perhaps you feel like you are in an oil press today. Are you experiencing dark, lonely days in the oil press of suffering? Are affliction, adversity, and trouble pressing in on you from all sides and you can find no way to escape? Perhaps people are persecuting you or saying all manner of evil against you falsely? If so, this is your opportunity to surrender your desires for justice to God and to allow these pressures to soften your heart and press out the overflowing oil of the grace and fullness of the love of God. Only this will empower you to love your enemies and bless them that curse you. This is the love of Christ that will deliver you from Satan's flies, which are reproducing their bitter, tormenting thoughts in your soul. This is the anointing of the Good Shepherd that will create a bountiful harvest of the fruits of God's Spirit in your life.

"Lo, I come: in the volume of the book it is written of me, I delight to do thy will. . . . He humbled Himself, and became obedient unto death, even the death of the cross . . . that He by the grace of God should taste death for every man. . . . Sacrifice and offering thou wouldest not, but a body hast thou prepared me . . . . Which is his body, the fulness of him that filleth all in all. . . . He that descended is the same also that ascended up far above all heavens, that he might fill all things. . . . We were pressed out of measure, above strength, insomuch that we despaired even of life. . . . I shall be anointed with fresh oil . . . to the measure of the gift of Christ . . . . In whom are hid all the treasures of wisdom and knowledge. . . . Therefore God, even thy God, hath anointed thee with the oil of gladness above thy fellows. . . . Love your enemies, bless them that curse you, do good to them that hate you . . . that ye may be the children of your Father which is in heaven. . . . And to know the love of Christ, which passeth knowledge, that ye might be filled with all the fulness of God. Now unto him that is able to do exceeding abundantly above all that we ask or think, according to the power that worketh in us" (Psalm 40:7–8; Philemon 2:8; Hebrews 2:9, 10:5; Ephesians 1:23; Colossians 1:19; II Corinthians 1:8; Ephesians 4:10; Psalm 92:10; Ephesians 4:7; Colossians 2:3; Hebrews 1:9; Matthew 5:44–45; Ephesians 3:19–20).

May these beautiful blessings of God be with you all the days of your life.

—Bob

CHAPTER ELEVEN

My Cup Overflows

When I heard the sound of running water, I knew that I'd forgotten to turn off the hose to the water trough. You know how it is. You get busy and you forget. At first all I could think of was the muddy mess around the trough, but then I realized that the overflow meant the animals had more than enough clean water to drink.

When David said, *"My cup overflows"* in Psalm 23, he wasn't talking about a cupful of spilled coffee. David was referring to a rocky depression that shepherds filled with water for their sheep. An overflowing "cup" meant that the water for the sheep was fresh and clean.

My first thought when I heard the trough overflowing was that I had a mess, but the abundance of fresh, clean water was really something good. Don't get discouraged about the messes in your life. They may contain blessings when you look for them. Don't be distracted by the mess. Rejoice over the blessing.

—Larry

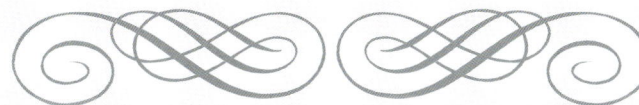

Assurance is seeing the good in difficult situations.

Doubt is being overcome by the messes of the world.

Isn't it interesting that when Larry heard the water running his first thought was that it was making a mess? But he stopped, chose to look past the mess, and realized that the running water was a blessing for the sheep. We become so easily distracted by the messes in our lives that we don't see the blessings surrounding us.

Good and bad things often happen in our lives simultaneously. I heard an old preacher say, "Good and evil run on parallel tracks, and they arrive at the station at the same time." We choose the track we focus on. Are you focusing on the messes in your life, or are you counting your blessings? If we focus on the blessings, we'll soon discover that our cup is overflowing with blessings we hadn't seen before.

> *If we follow the Good Shepherd, our cup will overflow with the refreshing love of God.*

DOES GOD'S LOVE OVERFLOW YOUR CUP?

When our cup is running over (Psalm 23:5), we are still seated at the King's table. We are in communion with one another, and we are anointed to bring the kingdom of God to people living in darkness. The anointing oil has stopped the tormenting flies of hurt and bitterness from crawling into our minds. Now, instead of focusing on the hurt caused by these enemies, we discover that our cup is overflowing with God's unconditional love for them.

Richard Wurmbrand told this story when he was in a Romanian prison: His cell mate woke him up one night and said: "Richard, I had a vision! Angels are transparent!" Richard couldn't understand what he meant until later that day when he was being tortured. As the prison guard whipped Richard's feet with a rubber hose, Richard envisioned an angel standing between them. As he looked through the angel, he saw the guard with all the potential for good and beauty that God created him to have. He felt such a deep love for him. The guard happened to look up and catch Richard's eye. He had never had someone look at him before with such love. He was so stunned that he stopped the whipping and stared at Richard. He then dropped the hose, fell to his knees, and asked Richard to forgive him. He never whipped him again. Such is the power of God's unconditional love.

We can love our enemies only when we love God first. And we can love God only when we understand that He first loved us even while we were yet His enemies. God looked upon us and saw all the potential good that He wants for us. When we look at our enemies, we are to look at them the same way God looks at us. We are to look past their sin to see all the good God wants for them. Our cup overflows and we will see in them *"whatsoever things are true, whatsoever things are honest, whatsoever things are just, whatsoever things are pure, whatsoever things are lovely, whatsoever things are of good report; if there be any virtue, and if there be any praise, think on these things"* (Philippians 4:8).

WHEN IS IT GOOD TO HAVE ENEMIES?

At first we thought our lives were plagued with problems and pain caused by others, but now we discover that the wounds God allowed us to experience are really blessings in disguise. These are opportunities to obey Christ's commands and bless those who hurt us. If no one ever wounded us, then we would have no enemies to love and we would never be able to obey this verse and experience the resulting blessing of an overflowing cup.

"Hear the word of the LORD, ye that tremble at his word; your brethren that hated you, that cast you out for my name's sake, said, Let the LORD be glorified: but he shall appear to your joy . . . If ye be reproached for the name of Christ, happy are ye; for the spirit of glory and of God resteth upon you: on their part he is evil spoken of, but on your part he is glorified" (Isaiah 66:5, I Peter 4:14).

WHAT ELSE DOES THE CUP REPRESENT?

The cup also may represent the plans God has for us. In Psalm 23:5, the word *cup* literally means "to hold together." It portrays the combined total of our lifelong experiences. It represents our lot in life: *"The Lord is the portion of mine inheritance and of my cup: thou maintainest my lot"* (Psalm 16:5). These experiences can be either joyous or adverse and are likened to a cup that God presents for us to drink. When the Psalmist wrote *"my cup overflows,"* he was not talking about a one-time event. He was talking about the whole of his life experiences. He was talking about his lot in life.

WILL YOU DRINK OF THE CUP GOD GIVES YOU?

When Jesus was in the Garden of Gethsemane, He spoke of this cup when He said, *"Father, if thou be willing, remove this cup from me: nevertheless not my will, but thine, be done"* (Luke 22:42). He could say this because He focused on the joy He would receive: *"Who for the joy that was set before him endured the cross, despising the shame, and is set down at the right hand of the throne of God"* (Hebrews 12:2).

When Richard Wurmbrand was cast into the Romanian prison, he drank from the cup God presented to him. He accepted his lot in life and chose to love his enemies unconditionally. When he was released, the lessons of love he had learned in the prison's torture cells overflowed into a worldwide ministry that has influenced thousands.

The words *runneth over* (Hebrew: *ravah*) mean "to be abundantly satisfied, to saturate." Notice how the following verses refer to a cup that overflows:

"For I have satiated the weary soul, and I have replenished every sorrowful soul . . . and thou shalt make them drink of the river of thy pleasures. For with thee is the fountain of life . . . And God is able to make all grace abound toward you; that ye, always having all sufficiency in all things, may abound to every good work" (Jeremiah 31:25, Psalm 36:8–9, II Corinthians 9:8).

This is the abundant life Jesus promised us: *"I am come that they might have life, and that they might have it more abundantly"* (John 10:10). Finally, we can experience this abundantly satisfying life and inner sense of well-being that is not influenced by our circumstances. Now we can experience the joy of an overflowing cup.

WHAT'S IN YOUR CUP?

Is your cup running over with abundant life? It's quite easy to determine what is in your cup. Whatever is in the cup will spill out when it is jostled. When things do not go according to your plans, do grace, kindness, gentleness, and mercy spill out, or does something else spill out? The Pharisees made it their life work to have a cup that looked beautiful and righteous on the outside, but God is concerned with what is inside: *"Man looketh on the outward appearance, but the LORD looketh on the heart"* (I Samuel 16:7).

Does your cup run over with God's unconditional love, joy, and peace? If not, will you purpose to *"take the cup of salvation, and call upon the name of the LORD"* (Psalm 116:13)?

—Bob

CHAPTER TWELVE

Goodness and Mercy

For Mother's Day some years ago I got my dear wife a couple bags of sheep manure as a Mother's Day present. Now I wasn't desperate or inconsiderate. I wasn't even being cheap. I knew exactly what my wife wanted and I knew what would delight her heart.

Sheep manure is just about the best fertilizer you can add to a flower garden. It doesn't burn like many fertilizers, and it doesn't contain as many weed seeds as do other forms of manure. Sheep droppings are simply good for flower gardens.

It is no wonder that the Psalmist wrote, *"Surely goodness and mercy will follow me all the days of my life."* Wherever the Good Shepherd led His sheep, the pastures flourished. The grazing sheep fertilized the fields with goodness.

—Larry

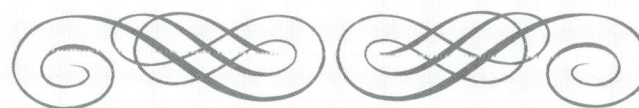

Goodness is bringing forth good things from fertile soil.

Barrenness is yielding to the hopelessness of a wasteland.

Larry related goodness and mercy to sheep manure, which perfectly fits the context of this Psalm. Sheep eat the luscious green grass of the high plateau, absorb the nutrition from it, and deposit the remains back onto the fields in the form of manure. When rain comes, the manure fertilizes the pasture, restoring its lush grass for the sheep that will follow.

In the same way, we receive the love of Christ that soothes our irritating thoughts of bitterness and temptation. And our newfound joy and peace overflow our lives in the form of goodness and mercy to others. This is the overflowing cup of abundant life.

> *Goodness and mercy will chase after you, pursue you, and overcome you.*

HOW WILL GOODNESS AND MERCY BENEFIT YOUR LIFE?

"Surely goodness and mercy shall follow me all the days of my life" (Psalm 23:6). The word *goodness* (Hebrew: *towb*) has three definitions: (1) "good understanding," (2) "excellent, prosperous, good, right, moral," and (3) "glad, joyful." When we are in the presence of God, goodness and mercy transform our entire soul: our mind, will, and emotions. The Hebrew word *towb* is highlighted in the following verses:

*"For thus saith the LORD . . . so will I bring upon them all the **good** that I have promised them . . . thou art that God, and thy words be true, and thou hast promised this **goodness** unto thy servant . . . If they obey and serve him, they shall spend their days in **prosperity**, and their years in pleasures . . . Who satisfieth thy mouth with **good** things; so that thy youth is renewed like the eagle's . . . The young lions do lack, and suffer hunger: but they that seek the LORD shall not want any **good** thing . . . For he satisfieth the longing soul, and filleth the hungry soul with **goodness** . . . So shalt thou find favour and **good** understanding in the sight of God and man" (Jeremiah 32:42, II Samuel 7:28, Job 36:11, Psalm 103:5, Psalm 34:10, Psalm 107:9, Proverbs 3:4).*

WHAT PLACE IN JERUSALEM WAS NAMED MERCY?

The Greek word for *mercy* is *bethesda*. It means "house of mercy, flowing water." In Jerusalem there was a pool called Bethesda. It was located just inside the Sheep Gate next to the sheep market. The pool had healing powers for those who entered it when the waters became troubled (John 5:1–9). Isn't it interesting that mercy is associated with healing? Mercy heals broken relationships. If we follow our Shepherd into the Holy City through the Sheep Gate, we can immerse ourselves in the pool of mercy and find that the troubled waters of broken relationships become healed.

HOW DO GOODNESS AND MERCY FOLLOW YOU?

Notice the manner in which goodness and mercy follow. The word *follow* (Hebrew: *radaph*) means "to pursue after, to chase, to hunt, run after and overcome." If we persevere in following the Good Shepherd on His paths of righteousness, goodness and mercy will chase after us, pursue us, and overcome us all the days of our lives.

Imagine being hunted down by a gang with these members in it: good understanding, joy, pleasantness, virtue, mercy, and loving kindness. They will chase us until they tackle us, yet we don't have to fear this gang. This gang has nothing but the best intentions toward us. We want this gang to follow us.

Or are you choosing to follow false shepherds by wandering on your own way? Are you trying to make life work in your own strength, according to your own plan? You won't be able to find the high plateau on your own. You must have the Good Shepherd to guide you. If you are lonely, troubled, weak, poor, or sorrowful, then you are a candidate for the abundant life—the life of following the Good Shepherd to the high plateau and the place He has prepared for you.

Humble yourself and cry out to Him. Surrender your will to Him and He will lead you—goodness and mercy will follow you all the days of your life.

—Bob

Let's review where our journey has taken us. The path of righteousness led us from the sunny plain, through the Valley of the Shadow of Death, and up to the high plateau (table). There we enjoyed fellowship with God and one another and were anointed with the oil of the Holy Spirit for God's service. The joy and love we received not only flows into us but now overflows onto everyone we meet. Goodness and mercy continue to chase after us all the days of our lives. Sounds like a blessed life of abundance, doesn't it?

WHERE ARE YOU NOW ON THE PATH OF RIGHTEOUSNESS?

Are you on the plain where life is going well for you? Is the Shepherd leading you through the Valley of the Shadow of Death? Or are you on the high plateau, sitting at the table He has prepared for you in the presence of your enemies? Is He anointing your head with the Holy Spirit and soothing the irritating, troubling thoughts you have toward your enemies? Is your cup overflowing with the love, joy, and peace of Christ? Are goodness and mercy pursuing and overcoming you so that you have good understanding and you are moral, kind, pleasant, and agreeable? Are you at the Pool of Bethesda soaking in the waters of restorative health?

"Because thy lovingkindness is better than life, my lips shall praise thee . . . How excellent is thy lovingkindness, O God! . . . They shall be abundantly satisfied with the fatness of thy house; and thou shalt make them drink of the river of thy pleasures. For with thee is the fountain of life: in thy light shall we see light. O continue thy lovingkindness unto them that know thee . . . Who redeemeth thy life from destruction; who crowneth thee with lovingkindness and tender mercies . . . I am the LORD which exercise lovingkindness, judgment, and righteousness, in the earth: for in these things I delight, saith the LORD . . . Thou wilt shew me the path of life: in thy presence is fulness of joy; at thy right hand there are pleasures for evermore."

Psalm 63:3; Psalm 36:7–10; Psalm 103:4; Jeremiah 9:24; Psalm 16:11

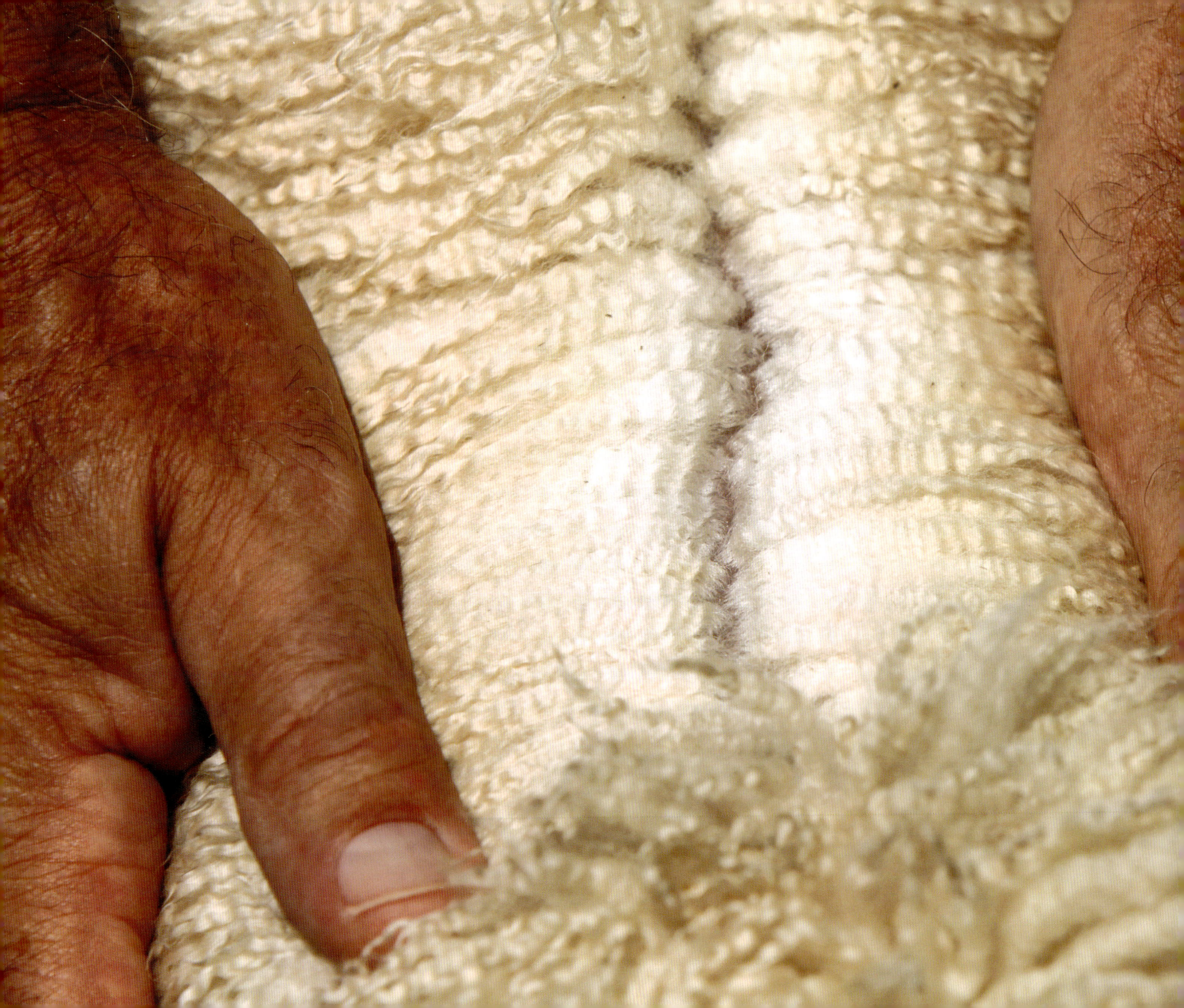

CHAPTER THIRTEEN

The Perfect Covering

It's such a delight to look out across the pasture and see our flock of sheep grazing on the lush green grass. They seem to be so "at home" in any kind of weather. Rain, cold, wind, snow—nothing seems to bother them. Their perfect covering of wool even protects them from the heat of the sun. In fact, their skin temperature can be 20 degrees cooler than what the thermometer reads.

It's no wonder that God chose lamb's wool as the perfect covering. Think about it! When Adam and Eve recognized their own nakedness, they tried to cover themselves with leaves. Leaves couldn't cover their guilt so God sacrificed an animal, most probably a lamb, and covered their nakedness with wool. What a beautiful picture of Jesus, the Lamb of God, who forgives our transgressions and covers our sin.

—Larry

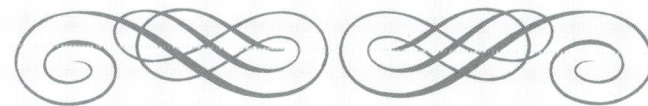

Innocence is having your shame covered.

Nakedness is having your shame revealed for all to see.

Larry described how the wool of a lamb is a perfect covering. It protects the lamb from rain, cold, wind, and snow. It even keeps the lamb cool during hot days. Not only is it a perfect covering for the lamb, but God saw that it was also a perfect covering for Adam and Eve.

> *That lamb died and shed its blood so they would be covered.*

WHY DIDN'T ADAM AND EVE KNOW THEY WERE NAKED?

Adam and Eve had to be covered after they sinned. Before they sinned they didn't even know they were naked. Why? Some say that human skin was designed by God to shine, thus keeping the naked surface of skin from being seen. The light that shone from the skin was its original covering. This is referenced in the book of Exodus when Moses came down from Mt. Sinai after being with God: *"And when Aaron and all the children of Israel saw Moses, behold, the skin of his face shone; and they were afraid to come nigh him" (Exodus 34:30).* It also refers to Jesus on the Mount of Transfiguration and the description of Christ found in the book of Revelation: *"And his face did shine as the sun, and his raiment was white as the light . . . and his countenance was as the sun shineth in his strength" (Matthew 17:2, Revelation 1:16).*

The Hebrew word for *countenance* means "in the presence of, before the face of, to turn towards." Thus, when Adam and Eve sinned, they turned their gaze away from God and onto themselves. One could say their countenances fell when they turned from being in God's presence. When the light of God was no longer reflected, they saw the surface of their skin and realized they were naked. Sin always has its focus on self and ego. The remedy for sin is to turn your eyes unto Jesus and come into His presence.

When Adam and Eve sinned, they tried to cover their nakedness with leaves (which represented their own righteous efforts). First of all, the leaves could not protect them from any inclement weather. Secondly, the leaves didn't even fully cover their nakedness. The Bible says they made "aprons" or "a girdle or belt." God saw that the covering of leaves was insufficient, so He personally made sure they were covered.

WHERE DID GOD GET THE CLOTHING TO COVER ADAM AND EVE?

Because God sacrificed one or more of the animals in the garden to cover Adam and Eve, He became the first priest to sacrifice an innocent animal. Though the Bible doesn't identify the kind of animal God sacrificed, many have assumed it was a lamb. A lamb would have been a perfect illustration of the Lamb of God who would be sacrificed to cover the sin of the whole world. Adam and Eve were covered with the lamb's skin itself, not just its wool. That lamb had to die and shed its blood in order to become a perfect, righteous covering.

Putting on righteousness as a covering is a central theme throughout the Bible. The Lord Jesus Christ is the perfect covering. We have to put Him on in order to enter into His presence. Because He covers our nakedness, we are no longer ashamed and our countenance will again shine just as it was created to shine: *"And they that be wise shall shine as the brightness of the firmament; and they that turn many to righteousness as the stars for ever and ever . . . Then shall the righteous shine forth as the sun in the kingdom of their Father. Who hath ears to hear, let him hear"* (Daniel 12:3, Matthew 13:43).

WHAT DID ADAM AND EVE DO WITH THE GARMENTS?

Adam and Eve had to put on the animal skins in order to have their nakedness and shame covered. In the same way, Jesus Christ was sacrificed for us. We, too, are commanded to put on the Lord Jesus Christ: *"But put ye on the Lord Jesus Christ, and make not provision for the flesh"* (Romans 13:14).

"I put on righteousness, and it clothed me: my judgment was as a robe and a diadem . . . I will greatly rejoice in the LORD, my soul shall be joyful in my God; for he hath clothed me with the garments of salvation, he hath covered me with the robe of righteousness, as a bridegroom decketh himself with ornaments, and as a bride adorneth herself with her jewels . . . For as many of you as have been baptized into Christ have put on Christ . . . And that ye put on the new man, which after God is created in righteousness and true holiness . . . If so be that being clothed we shall not be found naked . . . And have put on the new man, which is renewed in knowledge after the image of him that created him . . . Put on therefore, as the

elect of God, holy and beloved, bowels of mercies, kindness, humbleness of mind, meekness, longsuffering" (Job 29:14, Isaiah 61:10, Galatians 3:27, Ephesians 4:24, II Corinthians 5:3, Colossians 3:10, 12).

In Hebrew, the words *put ye on* literally mean "to sink into." Putting on Jesus Christ means to "sink into" His righteousness, which will not only cover our sin but also will cleanse us from all of our unrighteousness. When we put on the righteousness of Jesus, only then can we return to the Garden and come into the presence of our Holy God. Only then can we interact with God, just as Adam and Eve did in the Garden before they sinned.

May God's face shine upon you today, and may your countenance be lifted up.

—Bob

"And Abraham said, My son, God will provide himself a lamb for a burnt offering . . . he is brought as a lamb to the slaughter, and as a sheep before her shearers is dumb, so he openeth not his mouth . . . The next day John seeth Jesus coming unto him, and saith, Behold the Lamb of God, which taketh away the sin of the world . . . Saying with a loud voice, Worthy is the Lamb that was slain to receive power, and riches, and wisdom, and strength, and honour, and glory, and blessing . . . But with the precious blood of Christ, as of a lamb without blemish and without spot . . . These are they which came out of great tribulation, and have washed their robes, and made them white in the blood of the Lamb . . . For the Lamb which is in the midst of the throne shall feed them . . . And they overcame him by the blood of the Lamb, and by the word of their testimony; and they loved not their lives unto the death."

Genesis 22:8; Isaiah 53:7; John 1:29; Revelation 5:12; I Peter 1:19; Revelation 7:14, 17; Revelation 12:11

CHAPTER FOURTEEN

An Orphaned Lamb

It's next to impossible to persuade a ewe to adopt an orphaned lamb unless it smells right. If a lamb doesn't smell like one of her own, a ewe will butt it away and refuse to let it nurse.

So, to prepare an orphaned lamb for adoption, we place a sweater on a lamb with a healthy mom. Once the sweater has the scent of the accepted lamb, we turn it inside out and place it on the orphan. When the ewe smells the scent of her own lamb, she accepts the orphan because it smells right.

We are like orphaned lambs; the odor of our sin offends a righteous God. However, when we wear the covering of His own Son, Jesus, it is as if He sniffs us and smells the sweet fragrance of His True Son. Because Jesus was accepted and because we wear His covering, we are accepted into the family of God.

—Larry

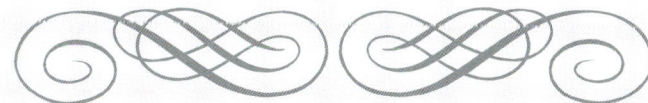

Acceptance is smelling like one of the family.

Abandonment is the cost of refusing God's covering.

This illustration from nature—how a ewe will adopt an orphaned lamb as her own—is amazing! The orphaned lamb must have the same scent as her own lamb's, or she will reject it. So, the shepherd first puts a wool sweater on her real lamb, and after a while he places that sweater on the orphan. The ewe smells her own lamb on the sweater and accepts the orphan. Only then will she nurse it and take care of it as her own.

This is a striking metaphor of our adoption by Jesus Christ. Paul says that those who are born again from above are adopted into God's family: *". . . But ye have received the Spirit of adoption, whereby we cry, Abba, Father . . . To redeem them that were under the law, that we might receive the adoption of sons . . . Having predestinated us unto the adoption of children by Jesus Christ to himself"* (Romans 8:15, Galatians 4:5, Ephesians 1:5).

WHAT DOES JESUS CHRIST SMELL LIKE?

The Bible describes Jesus Christ as having a sweet-smelling savor: *". . . Christ also hath loved us, and hath given himself for us an offering and a sacrifice to God for a sweetsmelling savour"* (Ephesians 5:2). The word *sweetsmelling* means "pleasing to God." The sacrifice of Christ produced a sweet smell that was pleasing and accepted by God. God adopts only those who have "put on" the Lord Jesus Christ: *"For as many of you as have been baptized into Christ have put on Christ"* (Galatians 3:27). When we "put on" the Lord Jesus Christ, we have His sweet-smelling savor on us: *"For we are unto God a sweet savour of Christ"* (II Corinthians 2:15). Just as the ewe accepts the orphaned lamb because the sweater it has on smells like her own lamb, God accepts us when we put on the righteousness of Christ and are covered with the sweet smell of His Son, Jesus.

HOW DID THE PRIESTS ILLUSTRATE "PUTTING ON CHRIST"?

In the Old Testament, God gave the priests a foretaste of the illustration of putting on righteousness when He required them to put on holy garments before entering into the holy place to offer sacrifice: *"He shall put on the holy linen coat, and he shall have the linen breeches upon his flesh, and shall be girded with a linen girdle, and with the linen mitre shall he be attired: these are holy garments . . . And he shall wash his flesh with water in the holy place, and put on his garments, and come forth, and offer his burnt offering, and the burnt offering of the people, and make an atonement for himself, and for the people"* (Leviticus 16:4, 24).

Isaiah prophesied that this requirement for the priest was an illustration of the righteousness of the coming Messiah: *"For he put on righteousness as a breastplate, and an helmet of salvation upon his head"* (Isaiah 59:17). Paul adds that we are to put on not only the breastplate of righteousness and helmet of salvation, but we are also to gird our loins with truth, shod our feet with the gospel of peace, protect our

> *God adopts only those who have "put on" the Lord Jesus Christ.*

body with the shield of faith, arm ourselves with the sword of the Spirit, and saturate ourselves in the sweet fragrance of prayer.

Christ was the great High Priest who put on His righteousness as a breastplate, and the sacrifice of His own life was accepted by God. Because of His sacrifice, if we put on Christ's righteousness, we can also put on the helmet of salvation. This is similar to God's covering the nakedness of Adam and Eve with the skin of the animal sacrifice. Before Adam and Eve could be covered, an animal had to be sacrificed. In the same way, God will cover us with the sacrifice of His Son and adopt us, but only if we are willing to put on Christ.

WHAT ARE THE LEGAL RIGHTS OF AN ADOPTED CHILD?

Adoption is a legal term. An orphaned child has no claim on the family who is adopting him. But once he is chosen and legally adopted, he has the same legal rights and responsibilities as a natural-born child in that family. It is only after adoption that he can claim the same rights of provision, protection, and inheritance as do the natural-born children. As an adopted child, he also has a responsibility to represent the family with honor and integrity.

When a servant was adopted by his master, the servant then became the master's son. This is why believers are no longer called servants to sin, but instead are called the sons of God.

"Ye have not chosen me, but I have chosen you . . . the LORD thy God hath chosen thee to be a special people unto himself, above all people that are upon the face of the earth . . . Wherefore thou art no more a servant, but a son; and if a son, then an heir of God through Christ . . . I have made a covenant with my chosen . . . Even unto them will I give in mine house and within my walls a place and a name better than of sons and of daughters: I will give them an everlasting name, that shall not be cut off . . . But as many as received him, to them gave he power to become the sons of God, even to them that believe on his name . . . The Spirit itself beareth witness with our spirit, that we are the children of God" (John 15:16, Deuteronomy 7:6, Galatians 4:7, Psalm 89:3, Isaiah 56:5, John 1:12, Romans 8:16).

DO YOU SMELL LIKE A FOLLOWER OF CHRIST?

If you are a legitimate child of God, there should be a family resemblance in your character. Is there evidence of that? Do you carry with you the scent of Christ's righteousness by forgiving those with whom you quarrel? Are you kind to your brothers, your sisters, your parents, and your spouse? Do you humble yourself before one another and repent when you have failed to act Christlike? Do you exhibit genuine love for one another? Ask one another if this is true about you.

By putting on Christ, the Bible says you will have also put on the armor of light, incorruption, immortality, and the new man. You will be different and will display fruits of the Spirit, which exemplify the love of Christ. May you walk (and smell) today like a child of the King!

—Bob

> *"The night is far spent, the day is at hand: let us therefore cast off the works of darkness, and let us put on the armor of light . . . And that ye put on the new man, which after God is created in righteousness and true holiness . . . Put on therefore, as the elect of God, holy and beloved, bowels of mercies, kindness, humbleness of mind, meekness, longsuffering; forbearing one another, and forgiving one another, if any man have a quarrel against any: even as Christ forgave you, so also do ye. And above all these things put on charity, which is the bond of perfectness . . . And walk in love, as Christ also hath loved us, and hath given himself for us an offering and a sacrifice to God for a sweet smelling savour . . . And he came near, and kissed him: and he smelled the smell of his raiment, and blessed him, and said, See, the smell of my son is as the smell of a field which the LORD hath blessed."*
>
> Romans 13:12, Ephesians 4:24, Colossians 3:12–14, Ephesians 5:2, Genesis 27:27

CHAPTER FIFTEEN

Wolves in Sheep's Clothing

To protect our sheep, we pasture llamas with the flock. Llamas bond closely with the sheep and know them so well that they can spot a fraud a mile away. It's not that they know so much about predators. It's that they know how to recognize one of their own and fiercely defend the ones they know against strange intruders.

Jesus said in Matthew 7 that false prophets come looking just like one of the flock. They wear a soft covering of respectability on the outside, but their real intent is to separate and devour. Jesus called them wolves in sheep's clothing.

It's that way in the world too. You don't have to know what a false prophet looks like to spot one. It might look like a sheep and smell like a sheep, but don't be deceived. You have only to know the truth and to know it so well that any deviation from the truth exposes the counterfeit.

—Larry

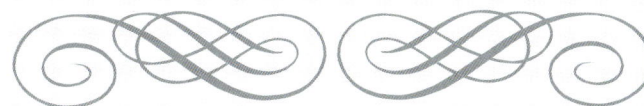

Truthfulness is revealing your real identity and intentions.

Deceptiveness is hiding under a counterfeit covering.

We just learned how an orphaned lamb is adopted by a mother ewe when it has the same scent as one of her own lambs. Satan took this wonderful idea and perverted it for his own harmful purposes. Instead of putting wool with the scent of a ewe's lamb on an orphaned lamb so it can be accepted and survive, Satan puts sheep's clothing on a wolf so it can be accepted into the flock of God, where it can devour and destroy: *"Beware of false prophets, which come to you in sheep's clothing, but inwardly they are ravening wolves" (Matthew 7:15)*.

HOW DOES A WOLF BECOME ACCEPTED BY A FLOCK OF SHEEP?

Satan loves to deceive. The sheep feel secure in their sheepfold when they are surrounded by other sheep. The wolf in sheep's clothing is accepted because he looks like one of the crowd. He talks like one of them and he even smells like one of them. They are oblivious to his intent. Having successfully infiltrated the flock of unwary sheep, the wolf will separate, scatter, and devour them from within.

HOW CAN WE RECOGNIZE WOLVES IN SHEEP'S CLOTHING?

Did you notice the wolf in sheep's clothing in the photo on the previous page? Look carefully, because he's not very easy to find. Satan wants us to look on the outward appearance. God wants us to look on the heart: *"For man looketh on the outward appearance, but the LORD looketh on the heart" (I Samuel 16:7)*. The Pharisees looked righteous on the outside, but God saw their hearts. Larry says the best way to identify a wolf in sheep's clothing is to know God, His character, and His ways so well that any deviation from this truth will alert our spirits to the presence of the impostor.

Bank tellers are trained to detect counterfeit bills the same way. In their training, they examine real money and become so familiar with the feel of it that they can discern the feel of a counterfeit bill immediately. They may not know what is wrong with it, but they sense that something isn't quite right.

The same is true in detecting a false shepherd. If you know the character of Jesus Christ well, you will immediately sense something wrong in the character of the false shepherd. Your spirit will be alerted no matter how outwardly convincing the deception may be. You may not understand what is wrong at first, but you'll discern that something is amiss. This is what it means to be mighty in Spirit, and it's contrasted to being mighty in intellect.

When we are mighty in Spirit, God's Spirit speaks directly to our spirit and gives us warning, even though we may not be able to explain what is wrong. Being mighty in Spirit is not dependent on our mental ability to comprehend the problem. Our spirit intuitively senses something is wrong.

When we are mighty in intellect, we depend on our reasoning and understanding to guide us. This may even override what God is speaking to our spirit.

> *The best way to identify a wolf in sheep's clothing is to know God.*

We will accept a warning only if we can understand why something is wrong. God's ways are often contrary to our natural common sense. Common sense is common to all men, but we need to have supernatural sense in order to make wise decisions in life: *"There is a way which seemeth right unto a man, but the end thereof are the ways of death . . . For my thoughts are not your thoughts, neither are your ways my ways, saith the LORD. For as the heavens are higher than the earth, so are my ways higher than your ways, and my thoughts than your thoughts" (Proverbs 14:12, Isaiah 55:8–9).*

HOW DOES A WOLF REVEAL HIS TRUE CHARACTER?

A wolf in sheep's clothing may have a very smooth, persuasive, and charismatic exterior. He may speak sympathetic words and draw in sheep with his concern. But he will speak evil of others behind their backs. He will sow discord among the brethren. He will insist on his own way of looking at things and will quarrel with those who have a different perspective. The wolf may look and sound like a sheep, but inside he is still a ravening wolf that desires to bite and devour the flock.

Scripture warns us that these wolves appear like sheep: *"Even so ye also outwardly appear righteous unto men, but within ye are full of hypocrisy and iniquity . . . The words of a talebearer are as wounds, and they go down into the innermost parts of the belly . . . Now I beseech you, brethren, mark them which cause divisions and offences contrary to the doctrine which ye have learned; and avoid them . . . This wisdom descendeth not from above, but is earthly, sensual, devilish. For where envying and strife is, there is confusion and every evil work . . . But if ye bite and devour one another, take heed that ye be not consumed one of another" (Matthew 23:28, Proverbs 26:22, Romans 16:17, James 3:15–16, Galatians 5:15).*

Wolves in your midst will speak smooth things and say what you want to hear. They convince you that you can decide for yourself what is best, but they are really luring you away from the protection of your Shepherd.

HOW DOES A CHRISTIAN REVEAL HIS TRUE CHARACTER?

The person who has put on the Lord Jesus Christ will exhibit His character in the following ways: *"Put on therefore, as the elect of God, holy and beloved, bowels of mercies, kindness, humbleness of mind, meekness, longsuffering; forbearing one another, and forgiving one another, if any man have a quarrel against any: even as Christ forgave you, so also do ye. And above all these things put on charity, which is the bond of perfectness" (Colossians 3:12–14).*

Jesus said that people will know that you are a Christian by the love you have for one another. Are you demonstrating that love of Christ to others, especially to people in your own home? Satan will do his best to attack that testimony by provoking family members to bite and devour one another. He's so good at being a wolf in sheep's clothing that many families don't even recognize him for who he is. *"For we wrestle not against flesh and blood, but against principalities, against powers, against the rulers of the darkness of this world, against spiritual wickedness in high places . . . Keep yourselves in the love of God" (Ephesians 6:12, Jude 1:21).*

—Bob

"For I know this, that after my departing shall grievous wolves enter in among you, not sparing the flock . . . And through covetousness shall they with feigned words make merchandise of you . . . Behold, I send you forth as sheep in the midst of wolves: be ye therefore wise as serpents, and harmless as doves . . . Take heed that no man deceive you . . . Children, obey your parents in all things: for this is well pleasing unto the Lord . . . see that ye love one another with a pure heart fervently."

Acts 20:29, II Peter 2:3, Matthew 10:16, Matthew 24:4, Colossians 3:20, I Peter 1:22

CHAPTER SIXTEEN

Silent Before the Shearers

When shearing a lamb, a shepherd simply slips his arms under a lamb's chest and sets it down gently on its rump. Once all four feet are off the ground, the lamb relaxes completely in his competent hands. A really good shepherd can shear a lamb in about a minute.

Goats, on the other hand, are a different matter. They resist everything, all the time, in every way. It's no wonder that Jesus used sheep and goats to portray the difference between the righteous and the rebellious.

In Matthew 25, Jesus explained that those who relax in His hands, like sheep, shall inherit the kingdom. But those who resist, like goats, shall be cast into everlasting punishment. Do you relax in the Shepherd's gentle hands, or do you kick against Him? Are you a sheep or a goat?

—Larry

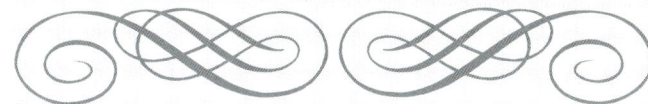

Yieldedness is relaxing in the hands of your Shepherd.

Resistance is struggling to take control of your life.

The difference between shearing a sheep and shearing a goat is that a sheep relaxes once it is in the shepherd's hands, whereas a goat "resists everything, all the time, and in every way." With this word picture in mind, Larry asks these questions: "Are you a sheep or a goat? Do you relax in the Shepherd's gentle hands and trust him, or do you kick against him?"

This illustration gives great insight into this verse: *"He was oppressed, and he was afflicted, yet he opened not his mouth: he is brought as a lamb to the slaughter, and as a sheep before her shearers is dumb, so he openeth not his mouth"* (Isaiah 53:7).

WHY DID JESUS KEEP SILENT?

Why would it have been wrong for Jesus to answer his accusers? Couldn't He have reasoned a little more with them, explained Himself, and tried to persuade them that they had it all wrong? After all, He was innocent and they were breaking God's law. Shouldn't He have defended Himself?

> *Jesus is the Lamb of God, silent and relaxed before the shearers.*

The difference between shearing sheep and goats explains why Jesus held His peace. He trusted that His Father was engineering His circumstances, even unto His death.

"But Jesus held his peace. And the high priest answered and said unto him, I adjure thee by the living God, that thou tell us whether thou be the Christ, the Son of God . . . And when he was accused of the chief priests and elders, he answered nothing. Then said Pilate unto him, Hearest thou not how many things they witness against thee? And he answered him to never a word; insomuch that the governor marveled greatly" (Matthew 26:63, Matthew 27:12–14).

ARE YOU PREPARED TO REMAIN SILENT WHEN FALSELY ACCUSED?

Have you ever been falsely accused by someone? Immediately you wanted to defend yourself. You wanted to be vindicated. You wanted people to believe you. But your efforts were all in vain.

If you haven't experienced this yet, then thank God, but be prepared. It is a certainty, if you are a follower of Jesus Christ, that you will be falsely accused sooner or later. When it happens, the pain will be severe. But a false accusation by a stranger hurts much less than a false accusation by a friend and brother in Christ.

"For it was not an enemy that reproached me; then I could have borne it: neither was it he that hated me that did magnify himself against me; then I would have hid myself from him: But it was thou, a man mine equal, my guide, and mine acquaintance. We took sweet counsel together, and walked unto the house of God in company . . . Yea, mine own familiar friend, in whom I trusted, which did eat of my bread, hath lifted up his heel against me" (Psalm 55:12–14, Psalm 41:9).

WILL YOU OBEY ALL OF THE COMMANDS OF JESUS?

Jesus Christ wants you to have every opportunity to obey His commands, and there are some commands you cannot obey unless someone falsely accuses you. Even Jesus, who never sinned, had lies and false accusations spread about him. That's why He said, *"Blessed are ye, when men shall revile you, and persecute you, and shall say all manner of evil against you falsely, for my sake" (Matthew 5:11).* Blessed? Yes, because unless you first have enemies who curse you, hate you, abuse you, and persecute you, you won't have any enemies to love! How will you act in these slanderous situations? Will you defend yourself or be silent like a sheep before its shearers, relaxed in the arms of Jesus? After all, God knows the whole truth, and His opinion is the only one that really matters.

King David was falsely accused. Many of his Psalms were written when King Saul was trying to kill him without cause. David had done nothing to deserve this, but he still had enemies who hated him:

"They that hate me without a cause are more than the hairs of mine head: they that would destroy me, being mine enemies wrongfully . . . They compassed me about also with words of hatred; and fought against me without a cause . . . Let the proud be ashamed; for they dealt perversely with me without a cause . . . Princes have persecuted me without a cause: but my heart standeth in awe of thy word" (Psalm 69:4, Psalm 109:3, Psalm 119:78, Psalm 119:161).

It is one thing to do something wrong and then suffer adverse consequences. You deserve what you get. But when you have done nothing to warrant accusations and people are talking about you behind your back, that can be especially disturbing. As our Good Shepherd leads us through the Valley of the Shadow of Death, He allows us to go through painful experiences. And then He tells us to *"rejoice and be exceedingly glad" (Matthew 5:12).* Why? Because these are wonderful opportunities that will lead us up to the table Jesus has prepared for us in the high pastures. If we love our enemies even when we are accused without cause, God will draw us into deeper intimacy with Himself. We will experience *"the fellowship of His sufferings" (Philippians 3:10).* and will find ourselves in the high pasture, above the cares of this world.

WHY DID JESUS ENDURE THE CROSS?

Jesus saw something beyond the cross: *"Who for the joy that was set before him endured the cross, despising the shame, and is set down at the right hand of the throne of God" (Hebrews 12:2).*

Do you see beyond affliction? Are you like a sheep that can relax in the Shearer's hands? Do you have confidence that God is still in control of your life? Can you bless someone when he curses you? Can you love someone when he hurts you? If not, you will be held in the bondage of bitterness and remain in the Valley of the Shadow of Death. You will be like the goat that resists the unjust circumstances every time, in every way, and demands justice instead of mercy. And you will have missed the opportunity to go to higher ground. Jesus is the Lamb of God, silent and relaxed before the shearers:

"Who, when he was reviled, reviled not again; when he suffered, he threatened not; but committed himself to him that judgeth righteously . . . Let us labour therefore to enter into that rest" (I Peter 2:23, Hebrews 4:11).

—Bob

CHAPTER SEVENTEEN

Loss Is Gain

Most of us have lost our baby teeth. When those teeth came out, we got a real sense that we were growing up.

Little lambs also lose their baby teeth as they grow. They're born with eight small "milk teeth." Two adult teeth replace two of these milk teeth each year. By counting the number of adult teeth and dividing by two you can tell a sheep's age.

We, too, can measure maturity—spiritual maturity—by what we lose and what we gain. Jesus said, *"Whoever wants to save his life will lose it, but whoever loses his life for me will gain it."*

So how mature are you? Have you lost your desire for worldly pleasure? Do you still demand your rights and grow bitter if you don't get your way? Or have you gained peace of mind, a gentle spirit, and joy that abounds in every circumstance? Remember, maturity is a matter of what you lose and what you gain.

—Larry

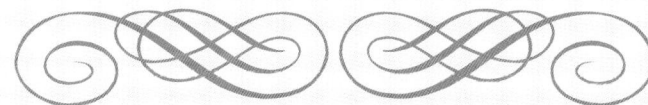

Maturity is giving up what you cannot keep.

Childishness is holding on to what you cannot keep.

Larry told us that we can tell the age of a lamb by counting its teeth. Every year a lamb will lose two baby teeth and gain two adult teeth. He concluded by saying, "Maturity is measured by what we lose and by what we gain." As we spiritually mature, we lose our spiritual baby teeth and gain spiritual adult teeth.

> *Maturity is measured by what we lose and by what we gain.*

Larry related that concept to this verse: *"For whosoever will save his life shall lose it: and whosoever will lose his life for my sake shall find it" (Matthew 16:25).* The word *save* (Greek: *sozo*) means "to preserve one who is in danger of destruction, to rescue." The word *life* (Greek: *psuche*) means "a moral being designed for eternal life." We were designed to live forever, but because of the curse of sin we are destined for destruction when we die. We are in need of being rescued. If we try to save ourselves, we will fail. The only way our lives can be saved from destruction is by losing them and surrendering them to Jesus. When that happens, we put on the Lord Jesus Christ (gain spiritual adult teeth), and we put away childish things (lose our spiritual baby teeth).

WHAT ARE SPIRITUAL BABY TEETH?

Scripture says, *"When I was a child, I spake as a child, I understood as a child, I thought as a child: but when I became a man, I put away childish things" (I Corinthians 13:11).* The word *childish* (Greek: *nepios*) simply means "untaught, not trained." Childish things are those things nobody has to teach you when you are a child. You naturally do them. Let's try to define these childish things that nobody has to teach a child but that should be put away as one matures in Christ.

WHAT DOES IT MEAN TO SPEAK AS A CHILD?

"My will be done!"

Children are by nature self-centered and demanding. It is almost comical to see a very small child stand up to his parents and demand that his will be done. It would be funny if it weren't so serious. When some children don't get their own way they throw temper tantrums. If left untrained, that little child will grow up to be an angry, demanding teenager and then an adult

who makes life miserable for everyone around him. This baby tooth must fall out if he is to mature in Christ.

"Out of the abundance of the heart the mouth speaketh . . . for childhood and youth are vanity . . . The way of a fool is right in his own eyes . . . There is a generation that are pure in their own eyes, and yet is not washed from their filthiness . . . What fruit had ye then in those things whereof ye are now ashamed? for the end of those things is death" (Matthew 12:34, Ecclesiastes 11:10, Proverbs 12:15, Proverbs 30:12, Romans 6:21).

Jesus illustrated spiritual maturity when He said: *"Father, if thou be willing, remove this cup from me: nevertheless not my will, but thine, be done . . . For I came down from heaven, not to do mine own will, but the will of him that sent me" (Luke 22:42, John 6:38).*

WHAT DOES IT MEAN TO UNDERSTAND AS A CHILD?

"Look at me!"

The word *understand* (Greek: *"pheneo"*) means "to be like-minded, to be on one's side." Children want to be noticed and accepted by others. This is not inherently wrong. God designed us to want others to give a good report about us. A child who doesn't mature in this area will become overly self-conscious, fearful of what people think, and willing to do anything to be accepted. Seeking popularity and prestige is childish and needs to be put away.

"The fear of man bringeth a snare . . . And fear not them which kill the body, but are not able to kill the soul: but rather fear him which is able to destroy both soul and body in hell . . . for I have transgressed the commandment of the LORD, and thy words: because I feared the people, and obeyed their voice" (Proverbs 29:25, Matthew 10:28, I Samuel 15:24).

Children need to be taught to fear the Lord and to seek His approval above all others. Children need to be trained to stand alone and to be courageous. A mature believer will suffer rejection and ridicule rather than deny the Lord and His ways.

"It is better to trust in the LORD than to put confidence in man . . . It is a faithful saying: For if we be dead with him, we shall also live with him: If we suffer, we shall also reign with him: if we deny him, he also will deny us" (Psalm 118:8, II Timothy 2:11–12).

WHAT DOES IT MEAN TO THINK AS A CHILD?

"Can you come out and play?"

Little children think life should always be fun. No one has to teach them this. If you give children a choice, they will choose to play over doing chores. Work is difficult. Fun is enjoyable! Children will choose what they like to do rather than what they ought to do. Succumbing to pleasure is a common trap childish people fall into. This is called hedonism. It declares that the purpose of life is to experience as much pleasure as possible. Its slogan is *"let us eat and drink; for tomorrow we shall die" (Isaiah 22:13).*

"Brethren, be not children in understanding . . . There is a way that seemeth right unto a man, but the end thereof are the ways of death . . . He that loveth pleasure shall be a poor man . . . Ye have lived in pleasure on the earth, and been wanton; ye have nourished your hearts, as in a day of slaughter" (I Corinthians 14:20, Proverbs 16:25, Proverbs 21:17, James 5:5).

The "baby tooth" of doing fun things should be replaced with the "adult tooth" of experiencing the joy of Christ through self-denial. If children are not taught to work and do well the things they don't like to do, they will not mature in Christ.

"Whatsoever thy hand findeth to do, do it with thy might . . . I die daily . . . For we which live are always delivered unto death for Jesus' sake, that the life also of Jesus might be made manifest in our mortal flesh . . . Set your affection on things above, not on things on the earth" (Ecclesiastes 9:10, I Corinthians 15:31, II Corinthians 4:11, Colossians 3:2).

Just as we can determine the maturity of a lamb by counting the number of teeth it has lost and gained, so can we determine our spiritual maturity by counting the childish things we have put away and seeing the character of Christ we have gained. Are there any childish things you need to lose?

—Bob

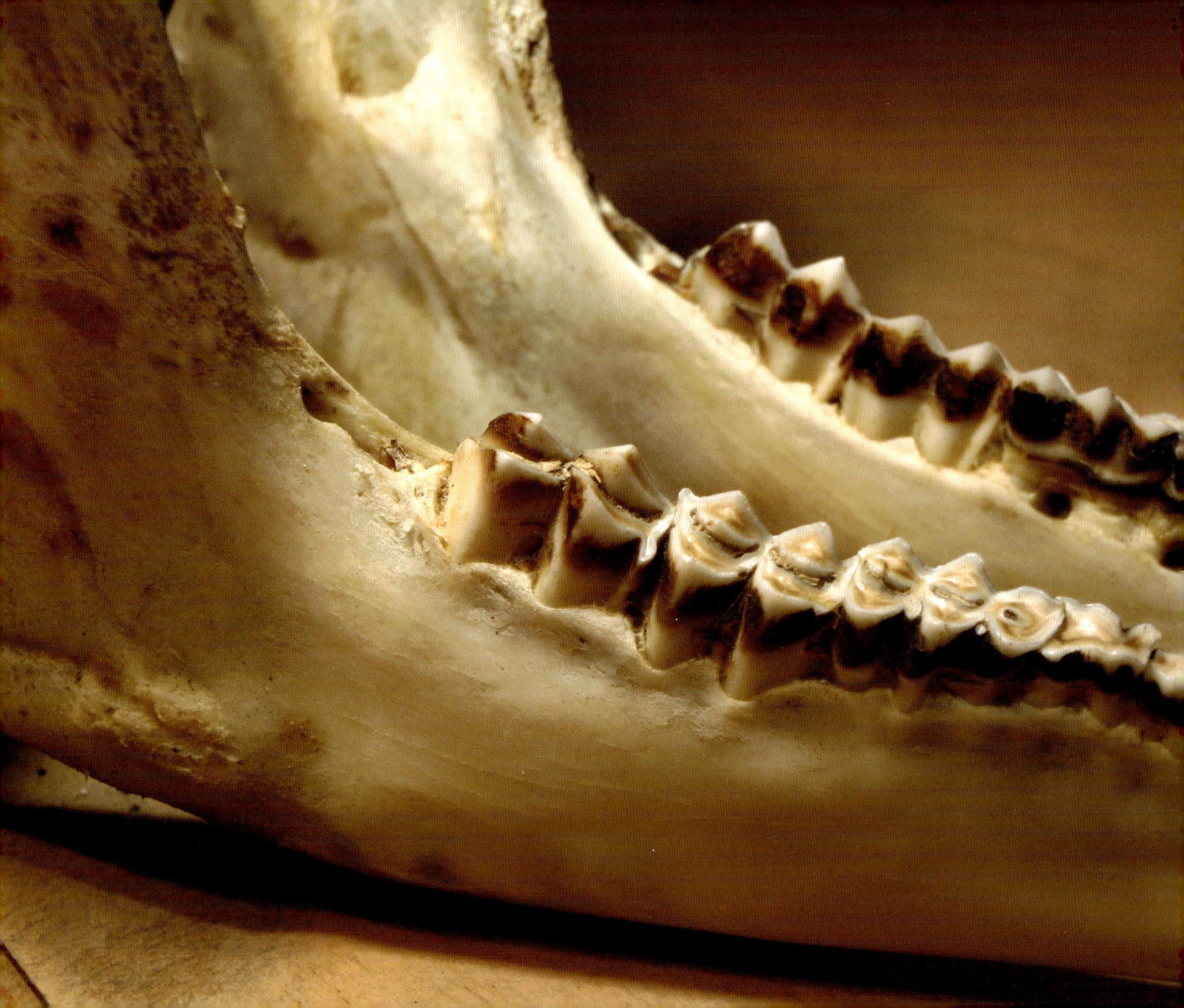

CHAPTER EIGHTEEN

Let Your Light Shine

Most sheep reach full size by about the age of two. By then they've lost half their milk teeth and their back molars are already showing signs of wear. Constant chewing broadens the contrasting lines between the hard white enamel and the softer dark dentine so that the relative contrast of light and dark layers reveals the age of sheep. The wider the dark layer, the more mature the sheep.

The opposite is true among Christians. As we grow in the Lord, we radiate more light and participate in less darkness. Paul wrote in Romans 13, *"Let us therefore cast off the works of darkness, and let us put on the armor of light."*

In the middle of the night even a small candle casts out the darkness. Give some thought to letting your light shine so that others may see in the darkness. It's the mature thing to do.

—Larry

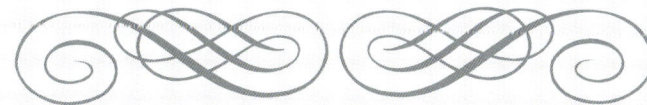

Radiance is showing increasing contrast to the things of the world.

Dullness is conforming to the things of the world.

Larry explained that as a sheep matures, the contrast in the layers between the enamel and the dentine of a sheep's teeth becomes more defined. The opposite is true of a person who matures spiritually. The contrast between darkness and light gets brighter as a Christian matures. As we put away childish things that are done in darkness, we walk out of the darkness into His marvelous light.

"For ye were sometimes darkness, but now are ye light in the Lord: walk as children of light" (Ephesians 5:8).

HOW DO WE WALK INTO THE LIGHT?

Do you remember when the sheep walked through the valley of the shadow of death? We also walk through dark valleys. In order to make it to the light at the other end of the valley, we must put away the darkness of self-will and fear. We must put away hatred toward our enemies and jealousy toward anyone. If we are to walk to the bright table that the Shepherd has prepared for us on the high plateau, we must show the love of Christ to our enemies.

"The people that walked in darkness have seen a great light: they that dwell in the land of the shadow of death, upon them hath the light shined . . . To give light to them that sit in darkness and in the shadow of death, to guide our feet into the way of peace . . . To open their eyes, and to turn them from darkness to light, and from the power of Satan unto God" (Isaiah 9:2, Luke 1:79, Acts 26:18).

WHAT HAPPENS TO US WHEN WE WALK IN THE LIGHT?

When a person walks in the light, he walks in the presence of God and the Lord's face shines upon him. This was illustrated in the life of Moses when he came down from Mt. Sinai: *"And it came to pass, when Moses came down from Mt. Sinai with the two tables of testimony in Moses' hand, when he came down from the mount, that Moses wist not that the skin of his face shone while he talked with him" (Exodus 34:29).*

The word *shone* (Hebrew: *qaran*) means "to send out rays." Why did Moses' face shine? His face shone because the Lord had spoken to Moses face to face: *"And the LORD spake unto Moses face to face, as a man speaketh unto his friend"* (Exodus 33:11). When we walk out of darkness and enter into the presence of God, we reflect the light of the Lord's countenance to everyone we meet.

WHAT MUST WE DO FOR OUR FACES TO SHINE?

The only way for a person's face to shine is to be in the presence of the Lord. For example, in the Garden of Eden, Adam spoke to God face to face, as a man speaks to his friend. Adam's whole body reflected the light of God like a mirror. Adam's face shone because he stood in the presence of God's light. When he sinned, his soul was darkened and his skin no longer reflected

the light of God. The covering of God's light vanished and Adam became aware of his own nakedness. Perhaps that is why God covered him with the lamb's skin; the lamb's skin replaced the covering of God's light.

> *Those who follow Christ are like flashlights that shine into the darkness of this world.*

Have you ever seen anyone whose face shone like that? It happened to me once. I was explaining the Gospel to a man whom I had just met. He was keenly interested and suddenly interrupted me in mid-sentence saying, "Did you know that your face is shining?" I explained to him that it must be the Spirit of God illuminating his heart. This man was able to see the reflected light of God, and that light cast out the darkness and made him receptive to the Gospel. The light penetrated his own darkness and allowed him to see. He surrendered his life to Jesus that very morning.

I thought about his comment later. This man's conversion occurred at a time when I had just repented over an issue in my life and was very conscious of my own weakness. God had forgiven me, but I didn't feel very spiritual at all, so it surprised me that this fellow said he could see my face shining. I couldn't understand how that could be until I heard the following explanation.

Science tells us that when an object draws twice as close to a light source, the intensity of the light increases four times. This means that God's light will not only reveal sin more clearly, but as God forgives that sin, the intensity of God's reflected light increases exponentially.

We can see light reflected in the lives of others, but we will not be aware of it appearing in our own lives. God designed it that way. True spirituality is not conscious of self; therefore a spiritual person will never think that he is a very spiritual person. But the moment we become conscious of our light shining, our focus turns away from God's presence and onto ourselves. Pride creeps in, and the light fades quickly. *"God resists the proud, but gives grace to the humble"* (I Peter 5:5).

Larry ended with a challenge, saying, "Let your light shine so others can see in the dark." The Hebrew word for *light* is *phos*, which means "anything emitting light, rays of light." It comes from the word *femi*, which means "to make known one's thoughts, or to declare." Sounds like a flashlight, doesn't it?

WOULD YOU LIKE TO BE A FLASHLIGHT FOR THE LORD?

If you would like to be a flashlight for the Lord, then declare what Jesus Christ has done for you. That is being a light in the darkness. Will you let your light shine so that people in the dark can see, repent of their dark deeds, and be filled with the light of God?

Jesus said, *"As long as I am in the world, I am the light of the world . . . he that followeth me shall not walk in darkness, but shall have the light of life . . . Ye are the light of the world. A city that is set on an hill cannot be hid"* (John 9:5, John 8:12, Matthew 5:14).

Those who follow Christ are like flashlights that shine light into the darkness of this world. The more mature you become, the more you will radiate light to others and the less you'll participate in works of darkness. Your light is the love of Christ.

—Bob

> *"Show forth the praises of him who hath called you out of darkness into his marvellous light . . . I will also give thee for a light to the Gentiles, that thou mayest be my salvation unto the end of the earth . . . He that saith he is in the light, and hateth his brother, is in darkness even until now. He that loveth his brother abideth in the light . . . if we walk in the light, as he is in the light, we have fellowship one with another . . . for the glory of God did lighten it, and the Lamb is the light thereof."*
>
> *I Peter 2:9, Isaiah 49:6, I John 2:9–10, I John 1:7, Revelation 21:23*

CHAPTER NINETEEN

Removing Temptation

You don't see many lambs with long tails. That's because most shepherds dock a lamb's tail when it is only a few days old.

We remove a lamb's tail so that it won't collect fecal wastes that can attract flies and cause maggots to grow in the lamb's wool. Docking keeps the lamb's rear end clean and free of offense.

Jesus talked about keeping ourselves free of offense in Matthew 5. He said that if your right hand causes you to sin, cut it off and throw it away—it is better for you to lose one part of your body than for your whole body to go into hell. In other words, it's better for a lamb to lose a tail than for it to suffer the offense of maggots. And, it's better for you and me to forfeit things that cause offense than to allow them to drag us into sin.

—Larry

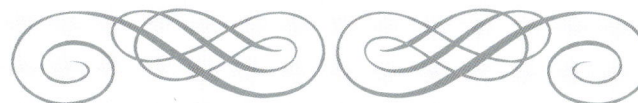

Freedom is experiencing the benefits of right choices.

Bondage is suffering the consequences of wrong choices.

Larry concludes his observations with this statement: "It's better for you and me to forfeit things that can cause offense, than to allow them to drag us into sin." He was speaking of removing a lamb's tail so it wouldn't have to suffer the offense of maggots. He referenced this verse: *"And if thy right hand offend thee, cut it off, and cast it from thee" (Matthew 5:30).*

WHY DOES A SHEPHERD DOCK A LAMB'S TAIL?

In this instance, the tail was not directly harming the lamb, but it provided an occasion for an offense to take place (maggots). So it was removed. In examining this verse of Scripture, it's fascinating to see the picture in the Greek word for *offend* (*skandalon*) which means "a stick, or a trigger of a trap or snare."

The trigger is what sets the snare. In this analogy, the lamb's tail is the trigger that attracts flies. If the tail is not cut off, particles of the lamb's dung will draw flies that lay eggs and hatch into maggots. The maggots grow on the tail and create great offense to the lamb. If the shepherd removes the tail (the trigger) then the maggots won't be able to torment the lamb. It's not a very hard decision for the shepherd. He simply removes the tail before the offense can even start. The lamb may endure a little discomfort for a moment, but it is spared pain, anguish, and suffering later. When the tail is removed, the trigger of the trap is also removed.

SHOULD WE CONSIDER CUTTING OFF ACTIVITIES FOR CHRIST?

If the love of Christ constrains us, we will cut off any activity that may damage our relationship with God for the same reason a shepherd cuts off a lamb's tail. I wonder if Paul was thinking about a lamb's tail when he said, *"I count all things but loss for the excellency of the knowledge of Christ Jesus my Lord: for whom I have suffered the loss of all things, and do count them but dung, that I may win Christ" (Philippians 3:8).*

WHAT MOTIVATES US TO CUT OFF ACTIVITIES?

The word *sin* means "to miss the mark" or "to wander from the way." If our goal is to be in the presence of God and to follow our Shepherd on our journey down the path of righteousness, then we will want to cut off anything that tempts us to break our fellowship with God.

Our love for God motivates us to cut off activities that cause us to wander away from Him.

If something draws us away from God into sin, then our goal is to return to His presence so we can again experience the fellowship of His peace, joy, and love. It is our love for God that motivates us to cut off all activities that cause us to wander away from Him: *"Love not the world, neither the things that are in the world. If any man love the world, the love of the Father is not in him" (I John 2:15).*

WHAT ARE OTHER EXAMPLES OF "CUTTING OFF"?

A farmer cuts off the branches of a tree. He does this for one of three reasons.

He cuts off a branch when it is diseased. Cutting off diseased branches is like cutting off carnal relationships and sinful habits that draw you away from the Lord's presence. Cut off the diseased branches now, or you will be cut off yourself: *"Behold therefore the goodness and severity of God: on them which fell, severity; but toward thee, goodness, if thou continue in his goodness: otherwise thou also shalt be cut off" (Romans 11:22).*

He cuts off a branch that doesn't bear fruit. Branches that don't bear fruit are like seemingly harmless amusements that distract us from the kingdom of God. The word *amuse* literally means "not thinking." To determine if something is harmless or not, we often ask the wrong question: "What's wrong with this activity?" Instead, we may want to ask, "What's right with this activity?" and "What kind of fruit does this activity bear?" *"Every branch in me that beareth not fruit he taketh away" (John 15:2a).*

He cuts off a branch in order to bring forth more fruit. As Christians, our choices in life are not so much between good and evil as they are between that which is good and that which is excellent, simply because of the brevity of time we have on earth. "*. . . And every branch that beareth fruit, he purgeth it, that it may bring forth more fruit*" *(John 15:2b).*

WHICH ANIMAL CUTS OFF HIS PAW TO FREE HIMSELF FROM BEING CAUGHT IN A TRAP?

When trapped, many animals actually cut off the part of the body that is snared so that they can escape and be free. A raccoon will actually chew off its paw if it is caught in a trap. A beaver whose paw becomes snared in an underwater trap will spin its body round and round until its limb snaps off. It is better for these animals to cut off their paw and be maimed than to be captured and killed by the trapper. But it would be far better if they didn't get trapped at all.

WHAT IS THE ONE THING GOD IS ASKING US TO CUT OFF?

God is asking us to cut off that which we hold most dear—our very lives—so that we can dwell with Him both now and in His eternal kingdom.

May God clearly reveal to you any areas you need to prayerfully and carefully cut out of your life. Remember, it's the love of Christ that motivates us. Let nothing stand between you and being with the God, who loves you so much that He died for you.

—Bob

"But none of these things move me, neither count I my life dear unto myself, so that I might finish my course with joy . . . For whosoever will save his life shall lose it: and whosoever will lose his life for my sake shall find it . . . whosoever shall lose his life shall preserve it . . . and he that loseth his life for my sake shall find it . . . He that loveth his life shall lose it; and he that hateth his life in this world shall keep it unto life eternal . . . For what shall it profit a man, if he shall gain the whole world, and lose his own soul? . . . whosoever he be of you that forsaketh not all that he hath, he cannot be my disciple . . . And he said to them all, If any man will come after me, let him deny himself, and take up his cross daily, and follow me . . . And they that are Christ's have crucified the flesh . . . For whosoever will save his life shall lose it; but whosoever shall lose his life for my sake and the gospel's, the same shall save it."

Acts 20:24, Matthew 16:25, Luke 17:33, Matthew 10:39, John 12:25, Mark 8:36, Luke 14:33, Luke 9:23, Galatians 5:24, Mark 8:35

CHAPTER TWENTY

All We Like Sheep

The more I get to know sheep, the more I'm certain that Isaiah was right when he wrote, *"All we like sheep have gone astray."*

For example, if left unattended, sheep get lost easily with no sense of finding their way home. If fenced, a sheep may actually strangle itself while reaching for grass that appears greener on the other side of the woven wire.

If there is a hole in the fence, sheep will find it. When separated from the rest of the flock they'll weary themselves trying hopelessly to get back in. And sheep eagerly follow the crowd, regardless of where they are headed. They seem to follow simply because they fear that they might miss out on something.

The next time you are tempted to stray or follow the crowd, or when the grass looks greener in someone else's pasture, think twice about Isaiah's words. Don't get yourself in trouble like our four-legged friends.

—Larry

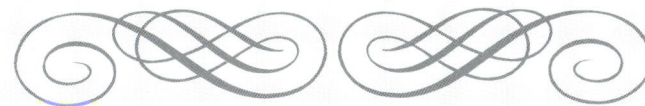

Submissiveness is yielding to the boundaries set by your Good Shepherd.

Waywardness is looking for holes in His fence.

In the first chapter of this book, "I Shall Not Want," we learned that sheep go astray because they're not content with what their shepherd provides for them. In this chapter we find that people are just like sheep. God likens His followers to sheep that have gone astray: *"All we like sheep have gone astray, we have turned every one to his own way"* (Isaiah 53:6). People, like sheep, go astray in more ways than we would ever care to admit.

John lists three ways that people go astray: *"For all that is in the world, the lust of the flesh, and the lust of the eyes, and the pride of life, is not of the Father, but is of the world"* (I John 2:16). Satan tempts us with things that feel good, things that look good, and the desire to be accepted.

> *If we're lost, we must cry out to the Shepherd to rescue us.*

HOW ARE WE LED ASTRAY BY THE THINGS THAT FEEL GOOD?

In chapter five, "Restoring My Soul," we learned that sheep become cast when they get too comfortable. They lose their balance, roll over too far, and can't get up. We, too, can get things out of balance in our lives. We enjoy too much of this and avoid too much of that. We do what is comfortable rather than what is right. We overeat, overspend, oversleep, overwork, and overdo just about everything. Why? Because it feels good. This may be one of the reasons Paul thought it important to admonish the Philippians to *"let your moderation be know unto all men"* (Philippians 4:5).

HOW ARE WE LED ASTRAY BY THE THINGS THAT LOOK GOOD?

We already have learned that the grass is not greener on the other side of the fence. It is an optical illusion, yet it causes us to be discontent. We search for ways to get what we want. We look for holes in the fence and quickly leave the safety of the sheepfold in search of greener pastures. When we eventually discover that the grass is not greener outside the fence, it is often too late to find our way back in. We are lost!

"I have gone astray like a lost sheep . . . My sheep wandered through all the mountains, and upon every high hill: yea, my flock was scattered upon all the face of the earth . . . For ye were as sheep going astray . . . Therefore snares are round about thee, and sudden fear troubleth thee . . . But godliness with contentment is great gain" (Psalm 119:176, Ezekiel 34:6, I Peter 2:25, Job 22:10, I Timothy 6:6).

Wanting what you don't have is the lust of the eyes. Have you ever coveted something you didn't need and later regretted getting it?

HOW ARE WE LED ASTRAY BY THE DESIRE TO BE ACCEPTED BY OTHERS?

Sheep eagerly follow a crowd. They are so concerned that they might miss out on something that they stampede without having any idea where they are headed. They run just because all the others are running. Bison also demonstrate this trait. When one bison begins running, the entire herd stampedes. They've even been known to follow one another off a cliff to their own destruction.

Have you ever seen people trying hard to fit in with their group? They do some things just to be accepted. They wear a certain style of clothes in order to be included. People can become so preoccupied with being accepted by those who appear to be in the lead that they knowingly do something wrong just to avoid being rejected.

Have you ever done something just because everybody else was doing it, even though you knew it was wrong? Did you suffer any consequences as a result of going astray? Pride motivates us to seek acceptance from others.

HOW DO WE WANDER AWAY WHEN LEFT UNATTENDED?

In Isaiah 53:6, the word *astray* (Hebrew: *taah*) means "a wandering of the mind, to cause to err, to stagger as if intoxicated, to mislead." Sheep begin to wander the moment the shepherd leaves them unattended. The moment we leave our minds unattended, our thoughts begin to wander. It is as if our minds become intoxicated—we stagger about, tossed by every lustful temptation, and we may do things we later regret.

To prevent their sheep from wandering, shepherds spend lots of time with them. They don't leave them unattended except when they are safely gathered together in a sheepfold. Could it be that we, too, need to guard our thoughts and gather them together into the sheepfold of our Shepherd? Scripture commands us to *"gird up the loins of your mind, be sober . . . Let your loins be girded about, and your lights burning . . . Stand therefore, having your loins girt about with truth . . . But the end of all things is at hand: be ye therefore sober, and watch unto prayer" (I Peter 1:13, Luke 12:35, Ephesians 6:14, I Peter 4:7).* Wandering thoughts tempt our flesh. Therefore, we must gird up these wandering thoughts and focus on God by reading, memorizing, and meditating on His Word.

WHY CAN'T WE FIND OUR WAY BACK ON OUR OWN?

Sheep go astray by wandering, seeking greener pastures, and following other sheep. In every case, once lost, they are incapable of finding their way back on their own. The same is true of us. Once we have allowed our minds to wander, indulged our lusts, or followed others into sin, we cannot find our way back on our own either. We need our loving Shepherd to find and rescue us. That's why the Good Shepherd left the ninety-nine and went searching for His lost sheep (Matthew 18:12).

A line in "Amazing Grace" says, "I once was lost, but now am found." Will you let Jesus find you? Will you plead for Him to rescue you? His arms are open wide. He is waiting to carry you home. He loves you with unconditional love, and He longs to be with you no matter how sinful you are. The love of God is so powerful it even makes sheep that have gone astray want to come home.

—Bob

"My people hath been lost sheep . . . I have gone astray like a lost sheep; seek thy servant . . . Call upon me in the day of trouble: I will deliver thee . . . Out of the depths have I cried unto thee, O LORD . . . Then they cried unto the LORD in their trouble, and he saved them out of their distresses . . . For ye were as sheep going astray; but are now returned unto the Shepherd and Bishop of your souls . . . I am not sent but unto the lost sheep of the house of Israel . . . For the Son of man is come to save that which was lost . . . For this my son was dead, and is alive again; he was lost, and is found. And they began to be merry."

Jeremiah 50:6, Psalm 119:176, Psalm 50:15, Psalm 130:1, Psalm 107:13, I Peter 2:25, Matthew 15:24, Matthew 18:11, Luke 15:24

ABOUT THE AUTHORS

Dr. Larry Guthrie is responsible for teaching and developing curriculum for Harvest Home Farm. He uses God's creation to teach about the Creator's invisible attributes, eternal power, and divine nature (Romans 1:20).

Larry is a former research assistant and writer for the Institute in Basic Life Principles. He has worked on publications such as *Character Sketches* and the Wisdom Booklets associated with the Advanced Training Institute International. Dr. Guthrie directed the Children's Institute, which offered character training and instruction in basic Biblical principles to children aged 6–12. Dr. Guthrie also served as Director of Curriculum Development for Character First! Education, a national nonprofit character training program for public schools with headquarters in Oklahoma City.

Larry is involved in Christian camping and served for a number of years at both Fort Wilderness and Camp Forest Springs in northern Wisconsin.

Larry is a graduate of the University of Illinois and taught seven years as a public school science teacher before becoming an Assistant Professor of Education at Indiana University Northwest. Larry and his wife Lois have two married children and seven grandchildren.

You can reach Larry through www.harvesthomefarm.org.

Robert Newhouse founded and has been the Executive Director of the TEACH Institute and Accrediting Association for twenty-eight years. The acronym TEACH stands for Teaching Effective Academics and Character at Home, and its mission is to assist families who are called by God to train their children at home.

In 1987, Bob and his wife, Bethany, were on the governor's task force that crafted the current compulsory education bill in Minnesota. TEACH is a recognized accrediting association that verifies the academic progress of home-educated students. Bob has also worked as an independent educational family consultant for twenty-eight years, turning the hearts of children to their fathers and the father's heart to his children (Malachi 4:6).

Bob is a graduate of the Minnesota State University Mankato, and he taught for four years at Faith Academy, a nondenominational Christian school, where he was also the Dean of Students. He is also the cofounder and former Dean of Students at Magdalen College in Minneapolis.

Bob and his wife Bethany live in Stillwater, Minnesota, and have five children and three grandchildren and counting.

You can reach Bob through www.teachinstitute.org.